JEWMOROUS

A Collection of
Stories Which Prove
I'm Full of SCHTICK!

Herman Lentz

I lovingly dedicate this book to my sons James and Jon, my daughter in-laws Jen and Allison, my grandchildren Leila, Maddie, Logan, Olivia, and Cameron, and especially to my muse, Thalia (who I would like to believe laughs at my stories when I am not looking).

Preface

Judaism can be traced back over 4000 years ago, when G-d made a covenant with Abraham that his lineage would become G-d's Chosen people.

While the history of the Jews is an extremely compelling story (and often brings into question why being "Chosen" is not the greatest thing in the world), it has absolutely nothing to do with my book.

The origin of *Jewmorous* is humbler and can be traced back to a conversation I had with my daughter-in-law, Allison. I made a joke, which I often do, and she didn't understand, which often happens when I talk to people. So I said, "It's just me attempting to be humorous."

Allison didn't hear me correctly. With a quizzical look on her face, she said, "You're trying to be Jewmorous? I don't get it."

I had just heard the greatest worst pun ever. Well, I'm Jewish and, in my opinion, I'm humorous. I knew I had the title for my book.

Definitions

Jew (jōō) – *noun* 1. An adherent of Judaism.
2. A descendant of the Hebrew people.

hu·mor - (hyōō´mər) *noun* 1. The quality of being amusing or comedic, especially as expressed in literature or speech.
2: the power to see or tell about the amusing side of things: a keen perception of the comic or the ridiculous.

Jew-morous – (jōō´mər-əs) *adjective*
1. How I view myself
(an opinion not always shared by others).

CONTENTS

JEWMOROUS

The Mati

After years of watching me suffer from migraine headaches, Thalia prepared a line chart to track my symptoms. After comparing the outbreaks of my migraines with the multitude of her family functions, we found that it was no statistical anomaly; there was a near-perfect correlation between the two events. Had she included the times she asked me to perform physical labor or go shopping with her, the lines would have overlapped perfectly.

My first migraine was in the summer of 1981. After our honeymoon, instead of heading to our apartment to start our new life together, we went to Thalia's parents' house. It was packed with more than forty people, who were still celebrating our nuptials a week later. Thalia is a first-generation Greek American, and I am a Long Island Jew. There are cultural idiosyncrasies I am still not totally accustomed to. At a Jewish wedding, once the waiters start breaking down the Viennese dessert table, everyone is pushing and shoving to be the first in line at the valet stand. Meanwhile, it had been a full week since the wedding and her family was still partying.

Shortly after we arrived at my in-laws' house, I got a terrible headache. At first I thought it was from the overpowering aroma of garlic and ouzo that permeated the air. It was unlike any headache I'd ever had before. I was led to a bedroom in the back of the house to lie down.

Another eccentricity of Greek culture is their belief in the "mati," or the evil eye. With a single malicious glance, a person can place a curse that can result in everything from slight dizziness to a debilitating headache or a string of bad luck. There are ways to ward off the mati. The best-known deterrent is to wear a talisman that has the power to ward off the evil eye. Spitting on an afflicted person three times is another method to prevent the curse. When Thalia and I were dating, I just assumed that some members of her family didn't like me because they all kept spitting on me. If someone compliments a baby too profusely, you must scratch the baby's bum to prevent the mati. If any of Thalia's female cousins wanted to scratch my bum instead of spitting on me, I certainly would've had no problem with that.

Everyone was convinced that my headache meant someone had cursed me with the mati. Why would anyone in Thalia's family want to give me the evil eye? A Long Island Jew marries a first-generation Greek Orthodox woman in a Unitarian ceremony—come on, it had to be a coincidence.

Luckily, there is a cure for the evil eye. The Greek version of an exorcism, called a Xematiasma, must be performed. This centuries-old secret ritual is handed down to a worthy family member of the opposite sex, who is sworn to secrecy. If they were to disclose the rite or perform it indiscriminately, they would lose their healing powers. It was my good fortune that Thalia's grandmother YiaYia and her mother's godmother Nona were in attendance. They were both revered members of this secret fraternity. YiaYia and Nona were cousins and had been rivals since their childhood days as peasant girls in a small village in Greece.

Now matriarchs in their seventies, they had been wearing black for close to forty years as tradition dictates. While I was sorry that they both lost their husbands at a young age, it did take the guesswork out of what to buy them for Christmas or their birthdays. YiaYia had been living in the States for the past twenty-five years. Her head was constantly tilted at a forty-five-degree angle, her folded hands had left a permanent indentation on her lap, and she was always clenching a crumpled, calcified Kleenex. Nona had remained in Greece and worked in the tobacco fields all her life. A robust woman, her face was etched like the ruins of the Acropolis, and her ever-present smile displayed the three random teeth scattered in her mouth.

As I lay in the back room in pain, YiaYia and Nona were fighting over who would have the honor of removing the mati. Although they fell just short of casting spells upon each other, it was a heated argument. Eventually, they compromised and decided to perform the ceremony simultaneously. When the old women came in to heal me, the forty other people in the house followed behind, jockeying for position in the doorway and peeking through windows to watch the spectacle.

As I prayed for the Angel of Death to come and take me away, I opened my eyes and saw two black-clad figures hovering over me, swaying back and forth, incoherently chanting, pouring salt on me, making the sign of the cross, and pressing pieces of bread against my forehead and then eating them. Oy vey! Thalia and I had dated for less than a year and had only been married for a week. I suddenly found myself defenseless, surrounded by relative strangers, and being treated like an appetizer dip. Where is the Jewish Defense League when you need them?

When an evil spirit leaves the afflicted, it enters the body of the person performing the ceremony. Of course they can't let an evil spirit stay inside them, so they have to expunge it. Normally, that consists of a couple of yawns, a cough or two, an occasional burp, and maybe even a fart. (Admittedly, those last two bodily functions aren't usually part of the cure and might have more to do with the age of the healer.) With a growing audience, these two childhood rivals had to prove that they had sucked more of the evil spirit out of me than the other. To my utter disbelief, they started gyrating, hacking, and spitting all over the room. The phlegm was flying. As soon as one spit out an unidentifiable object, the other had to dig deep into the recesses of her lungs and sinus cavity and find a way to top it.

When it was all over, the room looked like a crime scene. The innocent bystanders in the doorway were caught in the crossfire and were wiping saliva from their faces. Exhausted and spent, YiaYia and Nona retired to a bedroom to recover.

At last, the headache went away. The onlookers determined that the battle had been a draw. As I lay there covered in an assortment of bodily fluids, I was more than a tad freaked out. While I was appreciative of the effort YiaYia and Nona put into the ceremony, I credited the four Extra Strength Tylenol I took with playing a more significant role in my recovery.

Thalia, on the other hand, was convinced that the xematiasma had cured me. I contemplated my future. Did this mean that every time I got sick, Thalia would stand in front of a boiling cauldron chanting, "Double, double toil and trouble"? Where in New Jersey would she get eye of newt and toe of frog? Would I be forever subjected to superstitions and old wives' tales? Hadn't she heard about the healing powers of chicken soup? Why not just spray me with Windex?

Years later, I learned that Thalia's family hadn't kept celebrating for a week because of their culture. They just like to party.

I Am Not a Hugger

I am the black sheep child of a black sheep family. If you follow the axiom that two wrongs don't make a right, I'm screwed. However, I prefer to adhere to the mathematical equation that two negatives make a positive.

Growing up, I was not exposed to a lot of cousins or kinfolk. Lentz family reunions consisted of relatives sitting around a conference table as an attorney reads the terms of a last will and testament. To compound the situation, my sister was an only child, so I was never a hugger or a huggee.

There is also a cultural component that comes into play: while European Jews might be more demonstrative than the Amish, we pale in comparison to almost everyone else. Perhaps because they were constantly being hounded by Cossacks and just about every other ethnic group in Europe, my forebearers didn't have the time to develop their expressive skills. In fact, it is rumored that ultra-Orthodox Jews are so shy that they perform the sexual act with a sheet with a hole in it between them. While I don't believe that's true, it probably has less to do with modesty and more to do with dry cleaning bills.

So imagine my culture shock when I married into an extended, overly affectionate Greek family. Not only are any blood relations included in every family gathering, but even godparents and their siblings are considered part of the inner circle. Greek families are like Banyan trees, with intertwined branches that extend out in all directions.

Greeks greet each other with a hug and kiss. Male to female, female to female, male to male, and in some remote villages, male to sheep. It doesn't matter. But a quick hug and a kiss is not enough; no, the ritual consists of a hug and kiss on both cheeks. First they kiss your left cheek, and as they move across, they pause in front of your nose just long enough to exhale decades of garlic before kissing the other cheek. I found the feel of a mustache brushing against my cheek a tad disconcerting, but it was even worse when the men would kiss me.

Every time we visited Greece, I wondered how an electrolysis and waxing franchise would fare. It would either make millions of drachmas or go bust. I've decided that a better idea would be a dress shop that only sells black dresses, and only in sizes XL to 5XL.

While I understand that men greeting other men with a hug and double kiss is an acceptable custom in Mediterranean countries, it is not so for Long Island Jews. I have witnessed many of these embraces, and some of them border on softcore porn. The things I have seen some of these men do are illegal in most southern states. When they are done "greeting" each other, they may as well finish it off by sharing a cigarette. Frankly, I am surprised that there are any little Greeks running around at all with all of this man-on-man kissing going on.

Tradition dictates that not only must you greet everyone with a hug and double kiss, but you also have to repeat the process to say goodbye to every single person. I just want to leave; I don't want to go through a procession of kissing, which will take twice as long as it should because of that damn second kiss.

Early in my marriage, I decided that I was not going to subject myself and my antiseptic ways to this absurd custom. I needed a solution. Someone mentioned that I should use an Irish Goodbye, which I learned involves just leaving without saying goodbye to anyone. This option had a lot of appeal, and I happily would have utilized this perfect way of departing, but then I remembered how easily Greeks can curse you with their evil eye. If I left a family function without saying goodbye to anyone, I would surely end up at Beth Israel Medical Center with a debilitating migraine.

Over the years, I tinkered and developed the Universal Goodbye. I start by standing in the exit door with only half of my torso through. Constantly scanning the area to ensure that the escape route is clear, I stick up my arm, wave, and yell, "Goodbye, everyone!" For dramatic effect, I pat my heart twice, kiss my fingertips, wave again, and then expeditiously duck out.

Thalia's father insists on doing the hug and kiss with me, so I have developed more moves than a young Muhammad Ali, bobbing and weaving to get out of the embrace. It got to the point that we did our own version of Greco-Jew wrestling. I would put all of my weight on my back foot and stick out my right arm for a good old-fashioned USA handshake. My father-in-law would grab my hand and try to pull me in for the hug and double cheek kiss. It all came down to who had more leverage in this tug-of-war. I joined a gym to work on my upper body strength. I felt bad for him; he just wanted to express a natural and loving emotion. So, after a number of years, I proposed a compromise. I will kiss and hug him on his birthday, his name day, New Year's Day, and a floating holiday to be determined.

The kiss-kiss has even crossed the Atlantic and is part of the greeting ritual for our neighbors to the north. Under normal circumstances, this would have no bearing on me, but Thalia is a Canuck. She was conceived in Greece, born in Canada, and when she was twenty-two, she legally (illegally?) crossed the border and immigrated to the States. While I'm no longer willing to schlepp to Canada, when we used to visit her extended family or friends in the Great White North, I was accosted yet again. My reluctance to turn the other cheek nearly caused an international incident several times, and despite my great head of hair, it made me the ugly American.

It turns out that this is not only a Greek and Canadian tradition, as I have the same issue with my gay friends. I have been enthusiastically embraced by the gay community. And why wouldn't I be, with my hair, boyish charm, and rapier-like wit? I'm sure they would love to turn me, but I am completely secure in my heterosexuality. Alas, gay greetings also consist of the hug and double kiss. After years of exposure therapy with Thalia's family, I am willing to do the hug and kiss on the cheek with my core group of gay friends.

Now I'm left with the problem of how to greet the myriad people they hang with. Do I go in for the hug? Is a handshake sufficient? Can I get away with a friendly head nod in acknowledgment? The proper protocol confounds me. Without fail, it turns into an awkward moment because I always read the situation incorrectly. In all fairness, how am I supposed to know whether this person even wants to hug and kiss me? Maybe he shares a similar aversion and would find the feel of my silky-soft, heterosexual skin brushing against his cheek to be unsettling. I guess it all depends; a Greek or Canadian gay man probably wouldn't have any issues, but a Jewish gay man from Long Island probably might.

I'm cursed. I just have to accept the fact that I am too damn irresistible. Unfortunately for me, Wiley hasn't published a *Hugging for Dummies* edition, so I don't know what to do. Deep down, I know how bad it looks when I display the flexibility and grace of the Tin Man before Dorothy started oiling his joints. Greeks and Canadians and gays, oh my!

Artificial Insemination

In 1986, Thalia and I were having trouble conceiving our first child. As it turned out, my swimmers were not of Olympic caliber. They congregated in the shallow end of the pool, wearing swimmies, goggles, and nose plugs. The best they could do was swim lazily in a circle before drowning. If salmon had the swimming skills of my sperm, my fellow Jews around the world would be eating bagels sans lox.

Before learning that my sperm had the energy of cardiac patients in the ICU, each month that we failed to get pregnant was another disappointment. As the months turned into a year, the pressure mounted. We read books on conception, listened to old wives' tales about positions, charted cycles, and monitored Thalia's temperature like a turkey. We were open to just about anything and we were relentless. The frequency of our attempts that year, while both fun and exhausting, made me think about thirteen-year-old me. I guess G-d really had heard my prayers and wishes.

After a year of fun and frustration, we finally decided to consult a fertility doctor. Back in 1986, artificial insemination was in its infancy, and the doctors who specialized in it were OBGYNs. They started by testing my semen, and the results were disappointing. I found out that all the money I spent on condoms over the years—ribbed, studded, lubricated, glow-in-the-dark, flavored, drowning in spermicide—was all a waste.

The doctor delicately informed us that we were unlikely to get pregnant the old-fashioned way and recommended artificial insemination. Recent medical innovations allowed my boys to be put right into the deep end of the pool, greatly increasing the odds of conception. To get started, the doctor needed a cup o' Herm sperm for the procedure. We wanted a baby, and I was willing to do anything.

"No problem, Doc. I'll whip up a batch at home and bring it in to the city."

But apparently, sperm has a shelf life, and if we stood a chance at seeing a second line on that pregnancy test, we needed the freshest possible sperm. If I sat in bumper-to-bumper traffic in the Lincoln Tunnel or got stuck in the usual New York City gridlock, my swimmers would drown. Instead, she wanted it to go from me, to a cup, to Thalia in real time.

"Seriously? In the office, Doc?"

It sounded terrible, but the more I thought about it, I knew I had ample practice in what was being requested of me. I didn't think it would be a problem.

On the big day, we arrived at the doctor's office and joined the dozen women in various degrees of pregnancy who were sitting in the waiting room. That room reeked of estrogen. I was proud of what I was doing; I was the Before picture in a room full of After shots. I even amused myself when I realized that, without any fear of being accused of lying or duplicity, I could say that I "gave at the office."

Finally, the nurse called my name. It was my time to shine. She handed me a specimen container that looked like it could hold a 7/11 Big Gulp and pointed me to the restroom, which happened to be connected to the waiting room.

I said, "It's cool, I don't have to pee first."

She shook her head, pointed to me, and then immediately to the restroom. I vehemently shook my head no, and she forcefully shook her head yes. Afraid of getting whiplash, I reluctantly entered the restroom.

In modern fertility clinics, they have private rooms for sample collection with magazines, videos, and, in my fantasies, hot Asian nurses to assist in the process. But back in 1986, I was in the only lavatory in an OBGYNs office full of pregnant women. A woman's body goes through so many changes as she experiences the miracle of creating life. The body contains extra fluid during pregnancy, and as the uterus expands and presses upon the urinary bladder, the expectant mother has to pee a lot and frequently. That day, there was one restroom, twelve pregnant women with bladders about to burst, and me with a specimen jug and a severe case of performance anxiety.

The first knock on the door killed whatever momentum I was developing. At the second knock, I said, "Okay, I need a minute." I pictured a queue of pregnant women waiting by the door and anxiously crossing their legs, which only made the task more difficult. Meanwhile, back in the examination room, Thalia's legs were getting cramped from being up in the air for so long.

I ignored the next knock on the door. Unfortunately, this led to a flashback of my teenage years when I frequently had to scream to my mother, "I'm in the bathroom! Leave me alone!" Don't the women realize that knocking on the door was making it harder on the one hand, and in the other hand, it was having the opposite effect? I pictured the receptionist putting down wee-wee pads.

Finally: mission accomplished! My relief was replaced with panic, as my cup did not runneth over. How much should there be? Is there enough? Should I add some water? Do I need to whip up another batch? If so, why couldn't I be in my teens again?

In my imagination, I triumphantly walked to the reception desk holding the cup in the air like it was baby Simba in *The Lion King*. All the preggos would get up, start swaying, and join me in singing "The Circle of Life." Instead, as I opened the door to the restroom, I was forced to pass a gauntlet of extremely pissed women. I wondered if they felt any compassion for me and my plight. If they could only overlook their own symptoms—nausea, vomiting, fatigue, hemorrhoids, varicose veins, heartburn, indigestion, stretch marks, yeast infections, and backaches—and feel my pain.

With total stealth, I handed the container to the receptionist and took the walk of shame back to the seating area with my eyes averted. I wasn't sure what to do. Normally after sex, even with myself, I would smoke a cigarette and then roll over and go to sleep. That obviously wasn't going to be possible.

As I took my seat, I considered that maybe they didn't know what I was actually doing in there. *Nah, how could they know? Maybe I should mention something about a bad burrito I had for dinner last night*. Explosive, debilitating diarrhea would be less embarrassing than jerking off in a public restroom. Feeling more confident, I stopped studying the floor and looked up and saw my specimen cup sitting on the top of the receptionist's desk for all to see. *Great.*

Then I was struck with a horrifying thought. In my haste to free up the restroom, my aim may not have been perfect. Could I have left some of me scattered on the floor, walls, or even the ceiling? I panicked as I thought that one of the pregnant women might slip and fall. I could only imagine the doctor in the ER saying, "You slipped on *what*? Where?"

The longer I sat there, the more I needed to pee. I mean, I really had to pee really, *really* badly. My bladder was fully dilated and I was ready to give birth to a lake. I knew better than to attempt a return trip to the restroom. I would be beaten like a piñata by a throng of angry pregnant women. I just had to try my best to hold it in.

After what felt like an eternity, the doctor finished the procedure and came out to greet me. I could feel twelve sets of eyes staring at me. We both knew what my hand had recently been up to, so I did not follow proper etiquette and declined to extend it to shake hers.

She told me that the procedure went well, and we will know soon enough. Great! To temper my expectations, she added that it doesn't always take the first time. Oy! If this first try was unsuccessful, she said that we could repeat this very expensive process again the following month. Oy vey! Since it often takes four or five attempts before it's successful, I realized that I might be spending a lot of time in that bathroom. I no longer felt the need to pee. Instead, I was fighting the urge to throw up.

Our story does have a happy ending, and I have to give myself a hand. One month later, we found out that one of my boys actually completed the last leg of the journey and made it to the finish line. Thalia was pregnant!

Despite the fact that conception began in a bathroom, it is purely coincidental that we named him Jon.

A Herman by Any Other Name

Fuck Peter Noone, the lead singer and founder of the pop group Herman's Hermits. In 1964, their first single, "I'm into Something Good," went to the top of the charts in both the UK and the US. In fact, it was something good for them, but it sucked for me. As if it weren't bad enough being a Herman, now I had to suffer the indignity of being called "Herman the Hermit." That was not the relief I had hoped for after being called "Herman the German," a moniker that got me into many a fight at Hebrew school. Of course, Hebrew school fights did not involve fisticuffs, but instead consisted of threatening to sue your adversary for everything they own.

Sadly for me, the Hermits were no one-hit wonder. Their next hit, "I'm Henry VIII, I Am," flew to number one and dominated the

AM airwaves for months. I found myself saddled with yet another nickname. I couldn't be a Willie or a Sam, no, I was "H-E-N-E-R-Y the Eighth." When those blasted Hermits continued to flourish, Linda Brown and I had to deal with the fallout from their next hit single, "Mrs. Brown You've Got a Lovely Daughter." Linda was anything but lovely; in fact, she was much bigger than me and even scared me a bit.

Considering this history, it shouldn't come as a surprise that I have some not-so-minor issues with my first name. Even my wife, the love of my life, hates it. Every time she says it, her face looks like she's coughing up a hairball. The irony is that her name is Thalia; how many Thalias have you met in your lifetime? Even in downtown Athens, for every half a million Marys you meet, you might run into one Thalia if you're lucky. Yet she is cool with her name and has issues with mine. Not that it's a momentum breaker, but it is a tad off-putting to hear Thalia scream out, "Hey, you! You're the best!" during moments of intimacy.

I have often been asked why the fuck I was named Herman. Well, my paternal grandfather was named Herman, and he died a month before I was born. I felt like getting a T-shirt that read, "My grandfather died and all I got was this lousy name." I didn't even inherit any of his monogrammed jewelry or cash. What a bum deal. I've heard that he was a warm and compassionate man, respected and truly loved by all, but I never knew him, so I have the right to be bitter.

Despite being handicapped with an atrocious name, the original Herman Lentz was a highly successful dress manufacturer with a high-end, couture line of women's clothing. Sadly, the company went out of business shortly after his passing. How different my life would have been if he had lived; the insults I have endured over the years only served to sharpen the edge of my rapier-like wit. Who knows? I might have turned out to be a nice person, sans sarcasm and snarky attitude. I could have been a contender. A contender for what, I don't know, but a contender nonetheless. If he had lived, I would have a normal name and I could have gone into the family business. Like my grandfather and father before me, I would be in ladies' garments today. Not that there is anything wrong with that.

My grandfather was the twenty-second and last child of my great-grandfather, who had eleven children with his first wife. When she passed, probably from sheer exhaustion, he was in his sixties. As was the tradition in Anatevka—underfed, overworked Anatevka—he entered an arranged marriage to a sixteen-year-old orphan with no prospects, who bore him another eleven children.

When I heard stories about him, I pictured a virile, Jewish, Charles Bronson type. When I finally saw a photograph of him, I was shocked to see that he was no more than five foot four, stooped over, with long, white hair and a flowing, white beard. I struggled to believe that this little thing sired twenty-two children. Apparently, he wasn't studying the Talmud every night. The only thing that distinguished this photo from that of every other elderly, Orthodox Jewish male was the wall-to-wall smile on his face. Well, I should say so! I am sure the same would not hold true for a picture of my great-grandmother.

I can't blame my parents for naming me Herman, nor can I blame the drunk driver who killed my grandfather a month before I was born. No, the culprit was that septuagenarian, the Yiddish Brahman bull stud himself, my great-grandfather. He must have started running out of good names after the seventh or eighth kid. By the time the twelfth or thirteenth came around, he probably didn't even care or remember their names. If the twenty-first child thought he had the shittiest name, he must have been enormously relieved when number twenty-two was named Herman.

I hate the sound of my name. When I sign an email or a letter, I just use the letter H, and if it's a business-related message, I will sign it with the slightly more formal "HL." I thought I would be the perfect candidate for a nickname, but alas, I never got a good one. It's so unfair that anyone with the last name Smith, the most common surname in the United States, gets the nickname Smitty. Why does everyone named Smith need a nickname? Do they sit at the family dinner table and say "Smitty, pass the potatoes." "Sure, Smitty, no problem." "Would you also like some potatoes, Smitty?"

I ended up with terrible, rhyming nicknames. For a while, I was "Herm the Germ." Being associated with a disease was not exactly my idea of a fun name, but that was much better than the name I heard as I was entering puberty: "Herm the Sperm." Just what every teenage boy wants: being associated with jizz!

I've always heard people say, "Jesus H. Christ." Was Jesus's middle name Herman? Just look at the similarities: we're both Jewish, my mother believed that she was a saint, and we are both misunderstood by the masses.

Perhaps I should be put on the endangered species list, as I am probably one of the few remaining Hermans. How many other Hermans have you met? I have only met six other Hermans in my lifetime, and unsurprisingly, they were all at least thirty years older than me. Every last one of them hated their name. It made me realize that my name didn't just suck now, it has sucked for generations.

I'll even go so far as to say that there should be a ban on any male name that begins with the letter H. Harold, Harvey, Horatio, Hector, Howard, Harry, and Hercules (if I were of Greek descent) are all terrible names, but even so, Herman is by far the worst. I've even taken abuse from the other H-named suckers. In college, I met a Harvey, and he had the fucking nerve to make fun of my name. A fucking Harvey! The sad part is that I took the mistreatment.

Long ago, I tried using my name to my advantage. In the annals of the worst barroom pickup lines of all time, I once tried, "I'm Her-Man, but if you're lucky, I could be Your-Man." Oy vey. Over the years, I've written about a multitude of embarrassing topics, including masturbation, sunburned genitalia, prostate exams, drug use, and bestiality, but that pickup line is probably the most embarrassing thing that I have revealed.

So, after years of self-loathing, I decided to change my name to David. I liked the versatility. Dave could be my business-casual name, I'd use David for formal occasions, and Davie would work for intimate moments with Thalia. My friends, realizing that my first name is my kryptonite, told me they would not call me Dave or David, and there was no way they would ever utter the word Davie. I abandoned the idea.

Some people argue that there are bigger problems in the world than being saddled with a bad name. Young Herman would disagree. While on the grade-school trip to the Museum of Natural History, everyone else was admiring the foot-long souvenir pencil with their name on it that they'd bought in the gift shop, but I was sitting alone on the bus, empty-handed and dejected. While all the other kids in the neighborhood had monogrammed license plates for their bicycles, mine was made of cardboard. I had scrawled my name in magic marker, but it quickly bled through because of the rain (or perchance, my tears).

Just when I thought things couldn't get any worse, on Thursday, September 24, 1964, *The Munsters* premiered on CBS. I didn't watch the first episode, but I figured something had to be up when I was taunted all day on Friday. The other kids kept asking me about Grandpa and my wife Lily. With horror, I watched the show on the following Thursday and realized that every Friday was going to be a bitch. Seventy fucking episodes of that show aired, and then a long run in syndication. Given the choice, I would have chosen Morticia Addams over Lily Munster any day. Despite my young age, Morticia speaking French really did something to me. *Oui, mon amour.*

So today, at the age of 66, I admit that I still have issues with my name. Well-meaning people always say that it's not that bad and then suggest, "Why don't you just go by your middle name?" I sarcastically slap my forehead in revelation and reply, "Wow, thank you! I never thought of that before. What a great idea! I could use my middle name instead. Thank you, thank you so much!" For one shining moment, they think they have aided their fellow man and have solved my life-long problem. How quickly their smiles fade as I tell them that my middle name is Adolf.

The Ring

When I go on vacation, I try to broaden my horizons. Like a sponge, I want to absorb as much of the history, art, and culture of an area as I can by visiting museums and historical sites. In fact, I usually read up on the country before I go; I've been known to correct the occasional tour guide on their historical faux pas. Thalia, on the other hand, wants to spend her vacations stimulating the local economy. There have been many a trip where we left Newark Airport with two pieces of luggage and have returned with three pieces of luggage and a few extra carry-ons.

In the true sense of compromise, we usually plan our vacations to places where both of our needs can be fulfilled. After touring Athens, we went to the Greek isle of Santorini. With blue domed churches, beautiful beaches, breathtaking sunset views, the sparkling Aegean Sea, and flowing wine, it's a romantic paradise. What more could anyone want?

Well, Thalia wanted all of that, but she also knew that in the 35.12 square miles that comprise Santorini, there are over one hundred jewelry stores. I know that fact because I obediently followed all of Thalia's commands and heeled, sat, and didn't speak as we visited each and every one. In addition to life, liberty, and the pursuit of happiness, my beautiful wife believes that her inalienable rights include buying a piece of jewelry during every vacation.

Thalia did not like the standard fare that she found in the majority of the jewelry stores, since they all had a collection of the same ordinary trinkets. In one store, however, she finally found a truly unique ring. She spent a considerable amount of time admiring it, and because I was eager to be put out of my misery, I suggested that she buy it. Not willing to be rushed, she decided that she wanted to peruse the rest of the stores, and if she didn't find anything else she liked, we would come back and get it. Unsurprisingly, the rest of our search proved futile, and the more she thought about that ring, the more she wanted it. This was the one ring she had to have.

It was burnt platinum and decorated with rubies and sapphires. Thalia being Thalia, she was already planning on replacing the gemstones with diamonds, which are not her birthstone, but she believes are her birthright. She was going to have that ring. She was obsessed, and nothing was going to stop her from possessing it. Hearing her go on and on about it, I could only assume it was forged in Middle Earth by Lord Sauron during the Second Age.

Unfortunately, she couldn't remember which store she found it in. So on a Tolkien-like adventure, we were on a quest to find the One Ring. We traveled on donkeys up centuries-old mountain passes, trekked through back alleys and bazaars, and rode in rickety, old taxis on winding cliffs. It was all for naught.

On our last day in Santorini, we headed for the last store on the list. In the village of Oia was the legendary Oia Castle, perched high on the caldera and built in the late fifteenth century. Now known for the best views of the sun setting over the sea, it is a tourist mecca, with hotels, bars, restaurants, and of course, jewelry stores.

With dusk approaching, we climbed up the mountain to the castle. The trail was clogged with tourists whose goal was to reach the top to watch the sunset. We were on a different mission: to reach the summit before all the shops closed. And as the crowds stood frozen, gasping at the beauty and splendor of the setting sun, Thalia recognized the store and fought her way through the throngs.

With the angels singing the "Hallelujah Chorus," we made it to the jewelry store in time. The One Ring would be hers. She rushed in and slipped it onto her finger, and then approached the counter to pay. On the wall above the register, I noticed a picture of the store owner with his arm around George W. Bush. Thalia and I have a sort of history with the former president, and I spotted a chance to get even with her for the past few days.

Larry David is my hero; I am a devotee. In an episode of *Curb Your Enthusiasm*, Larry was making out with an actress in her dressing room. As they were groping each other and making their way to her bed, Larry happened to spot a framed photo of President Bush on the end table. He instantly lost interest in her and the scene ended. Thalia has a love/hate relationship with Larry and is not a fan of George Bush at all, so after watching that episode, she applauded his decision. Apparently, she respected his integrity and the fact that he took a moral stand. She said, "How could Larry have anything to do with someone who is a friend of George Bush?" Despite how much I worship Larry David, I had difficulty with his decision. Short of a woman dressing in Nazi garb, not much would act as a deterrent to sex for me.

I stood in that jewelry store, eager to drop the bomb. I nudged Thalia and gleefully pointed at the picture. When she looked at it, the weight of the ring fell upon her. Thalia knew she had to part with the ring. It was the right thing to do; keeping it would only corrupt her.

However, the ring held a magical power over her. She couldn't get rid of it; she was obsessed with it. As she stood there, staring into the fires of Mt. Doom and the smirking face of George Bush, I wondered if she possessed Frodo's fortitude or the moral convictions of Larry David.

She took off the ring and placed it on the counter. I watched in stunned silence. The forces of good had triumphed, the spell had been broken, and she had gotten rid of the ring. But then, she looked at the store owner, leaned in, and asked him what sort of discount he'd give her if she paid in cash.

On our flight home to Newark, I awoke from a Dramamine-induced sleep to see Thalia holding her hand in front of her face, admiring her new ring. I can't be sure because I was dazed and groggy, but I believe I heard her saying, "My precious . . ."

My Alter Ego

I lead a double life. By day, I am disguised as Herman Lentz, a mild-mannered, serious, rule-following Chief Compliance Officer for an investment advisory firm. At night, I remove my filters and transform into Sarcasticman, fighting the never-ending battle for humor, snarkiness, and the satirical way.

As a kid, I never understood why no one could tell that Clark Kent was Superman just because he put on a pair of glasses and a suit. Seriously, they were reporters for a major metropolitan newspaper; how could they be that clueless? I now realize that by muzzling my sense of humor at work, no one in the office knows my true identity or just how caustic I can be. Are my coworkers as dense as the staff at the Daily Planet, or is my disguise just that good?

Working my way up the corporate ladder, I had to learn how to control my powers. Sometimes I didn't know my own strength and took things too far. At a former job, Howard, the senior VP, got caught in a torrential downpour and was soaked to the bone. Steven, the owner of the company, had an extra suit in his office and lent it to Howard. Later that day, all the executives were in the conference room for a meeting. Howard walked in wearing Steven's suit, and Steven complimented Howard on how good he looked in it. Without thinking of the consequences, Sarcasticman blurted out, "We all know that Howard has been trying to get into your pants for years."

The silence was deafening. The other executives fled the room like rats off a sinking ship. Only Howard, Steven, and I remained. With both of them glaring at me but neither saying a word, I slowly got up from the conference table and walked toward my office. I figured I would first stop by the supply room to grab a bankers box to put my belongings in, and I started working on a palatable way to explain to Thalia why I got fired.

Unbeknownst to me, my line spread throughout the office like wildfire. As I walked through the hallway, a slow clap started, and then it multiplied and grew into thunderous applause. It was fucking worth it.

Surprisingly, I was not fired. Unsurprisingly, I was excluded from future staff meetings.

In my current position as Chief Compliance Officer, I play a crucial role in fostering the integrity of the securities industry. I have a fiduciary and regulatory obligation under the Investment Act of 1940 to oversee the policies and procedures of the firm to prevent violations from occurring, detect violations that have occurred, and promptly correct those violations. These are all responsibilities I take very seriously. When faced with daily inane conversations, I fight the urge to run into the proverbial phone booth and morph into my alter ego. However, I know the demands of my role—I must be a pillar of morals and proper conduct. To make matters worse, the level of humor amongst the staff is childish at best.

Like Superman, who adheres to a strict moral code and will not kill, I also adhere to a code: I will not snark the weak or infirmed. My problem is that the people in my office are ironically weak and comedically challenged. My code is killing me. But alas, the standard office repartee of fart jokes is my kryptonite. In the office, my wit is as sharp as a dull butter knife, and I am unable to participate in the mind-numbing stench of grade-school, locker-room humor.

My attempts to raise the level of wit have been unsuccessful and have only ostracized me from my coworkers. If we were in medieval times, bards would roam the countryside singing praises to the hilarious lines I craft, but in my office, those same lines crash and burn, only further distancing me from the common folk. So I keep quiet. I greatly amuse myself with my own private thoughts, but I still struggle to hold my tongue. It is an immense daily battle.

Recently, a coworker and I were chatting by the infamous watercooler. I would like to say that Debbie is in her mid- to late thirties, but I cannot, as that would be a direct violation of the company's human resources policies. Nor can I say that she is very attractive, as that would be sexist. So I will merely describe her as what I believe to be an adult female employee with nondescript looks.

As we concluded our business-related conversation, I said, "I had a terrible weekend. My wife wanted me to perform feats of physical labor around the house."

Debbie replied, "I love doing things around the house."

"Well, I'm Jewish, and as it is written, my people shall not partake in physical labor."

"That's funny! I understand, my husband is Jewish, and he is the same way."

"That makes sense. He probably suffers from assemblexia, a disease that afflicts people of Semitic backgrounds. It's a genetic disorder that prevents Jews from following written instructions or doing anything that requires exertion."

She chuckled. "I don't mind the effort. I enjoy yard work and fixing and building things. My problem is that my husband supervises and complains. I was laying . . ." she paused with a devilish look on her face, ". . . tile this weekend, and he started to bitch that the first row of tile was too far from the wall."

I was a little taken aback by her pregnant pause, so I asked, "Well, was it?"

"I was a c—hair off. Only a c—hair off and he was complaining!"

And then . . . Faster than a Borscht-Belt comic. More caustic than it ever calls for. Able to insult anyone with a biting remark. It's an asshole, it's an insensitive jerk, it's Sarcasticman! Standing there with my hands on my hips, chin aloft, and hair blowing in the wind, Sarcasticman was ready to enter the fray.

I knew that I had to navigate the situation carefully. How far can Sarcasticman go without crossing the line? She was the one who introduced a c—hair into the conversation—game on.

I said, "Just a c—hair off?"

Debbie went on a tirade about c—hair this and c—hair that, saying it at least six times in under a minute.

Feigning ignorance, I said, "Debbie, I'm sorry, I have no idea what you're talking about. My assemblexia might be in remission, but I guess you're using an industry term because I don't know what a c–hair is."

Adroitly handled, I thought. *HR would be proud. Let's see her get out of this one.*

Debbie looked at me, shook her head, and said, "You know, a c–hair." With both hands, she pointed to her pubic region.

Metaphorical beads of sweat were pouring down my brow. My knees were shaking. I had a thousand zingers cued up and ready to fly, but as Chief Compliance Officer, I couldn't say a single one of them. So, muttering to myself, I walked away.

Had I not been shackled by my role, my alter ego would have been able to make an appearance in all his glory. He would have responded, "Well, I became sexually active in the 1970s, and back then, a c–hair off could have been two or three inches from the wall. Maybe your husband was right!"

Fifty Shades of Gray

I am colorblind. It's impossible to explain to the "color able" what it's like to be color challenged. I see a color, but I don't know what it is, I can't differentiate between similar shades, and I have no sense of color coordination.

I don't want or need your pity. It's not as though I have a terrible disease. Aside from occasionally wearing a funky ensemble, no one would know of my affliction. There is no telethon or major fundraiser for colorblindness. Can you imagine a Colorblind Walk for the Cure? No one would even make it across the street because they wouldn't be able to tell when the light had changed from red to green.

Being colorblind might have even saved my life. During the drug-fueled '70s, I didn't bother experimenting with hallucinogens. What was the point in taking LSD and saying, "Far out, man," as I tripped on all the different shades of gray?

Thalia refuses to believe that I'm colorblind; she just thinks I'm lazy and don't want to go shopping with her (true and true). My color-blindness and my total lack of artistic vision frequently frustrate her. As she contemplates the kaleidoscope of a design in her head, she is unable to share any of it with me, not that I would have a say in the final outcome anyway. While I can't connect the dots in her thought patterns, her process fascinates me just the same.

I didn't learn that I was colorblind until I was fourteen years old. Before that, everybody just thought that I was a little slow. In fact, I almost failed kindergarten because of it. In the first month of kinder-garten, everyone was asked to bring a fall foliage collage to school. All my leaves were brown and dead. When other kids asked me for a green crayon, I would give them a red or brown one.

As I got older, my outfits never matched. The Irish would stare at me with disdain on St. Patrick's Day, trying to figure out why I was wearing brown and red. I never won a game of Twister. My abysmal grades in art class dragged down my GPA.

Then, at the impressionable age of fourteen, I went to the school nurse's office for an annual physical. She handed me a book and asked me to read the numbers inside the colored circles. I flipped through the entire book and said, "Someone sold you a bum book. There's nothing here."

With a very serious look, she sent me to the head nurse's office, who said, "I'm afraid I have some bad news. You're colorblind, Mr. Lentz."

"Okay. Anything else?"

She explained that there are two types of colorblindness: red/green and blue/yellow. It seemed that I had the red/green variety. She told me that it only affects men, but women carry the colorblindness gene and pass it on to their offspring. I couldn't wait to get home and spring this on my mother.

Very solemnly, the nurse said, "Herman, you can never become an electrician."

I guess she doesn't know that I'm Jewish. This is a nonissue, I thought.

"And because of the color-coded instrument panels, you can't be an airline pilot."

I am content with being a passenger, thank you very much.

"Or a police officer."

I can just picture it now. "I told you the perp was wearing a green shirt."

"Nor can you become a doctor."

Hmm. That one stings a bit.

There comes a time on the road to manhood when every boy has to face his demons. I thought that this news finally gave me the opening I needed. I would be venturing into unchartered territory to take on the master. Having been subject to a lifetime of my mother's guilt trips, I was eager to make the guilt-er become the guilt-ee. I rushed home.

I burst through the door and said, "Mom, I just found out I'm colorblind."

Flatly, she said, "No you're not."

"What do you mean I'm not? I took the test and failed, Mom."

"It's the teacher's fault. We'll get you a tutor, you'll study harder, and then you can take the test again."

"It doesn't work that way. Not only am I colorblind, but it's your fault. You carry the gene for colorblindness. Now I can never fulfill my lifelong dream of becoming a doctor."

"You're not colorblind, you're just slow. And seriously? You, a doctor? You're not even a good patient! The nurse should have checked your head instead of your eyes."

Oy vey. The master has won again.

After college, I rented an apartment with one of my former roommates. One major challenge for the colorblind is selecting appropriate clothes for work. To address this issue, I made an index card for each suit. I only wore solid white or blue shirts, and on the inside label of each tie, I wrote a number. I used the index cards to help me know which ties worked with each shirt and suit combo. For example:

NAVY SUIT

Shirt	Tie
White	1, 6, 8, 9, 11, 12, 14
Blue	2, 3, 5, 7, 9, 12, 15

One night, when I was out of the apartment, a bunch of my friends decided to screw with my index cards. They turned ones into nines and sixes into eights. I didn't notice the change for a couple of weeks. I wondered why people were snickering at me more than usual, and eventually, I discovered that my favorite tie was not assigned to the proper suit.

I faced a dilemma. Should I:

a) Ask my mother to come to my apartment and redo the index cards. (The doorman had a picture of her with a big red X, or maybe it was a brown or green X.)

b) Bring all my suits and ties to her home and spend an afternoon with her. (She still hadn't forgiven me for blaming my colorblindness on her, or the many other atrocities I have apparently committed.)

c) Buy a whole new wardrobe.

Well, it was off to Macy's.

Card Junkie

"Hi, my name is Herman, and I am a holiday card junkie."

My struggles with holiday cards and my subsequent descent into card hell began innocently enough in December 1987. To paraphrase the words of every contestant on *Wheel of Fortune*, I had a beautiful wife and two wonderful kids. Why wouldn't I want to share my happiness with the world? I was young and curious, so I decided to experiment with sending out a holiday picture card of my own. A lot of people were doing it. *It can't hurt to try once*, I told myself.

My first card featured Jimmy and Jonathon wearing antlers and red Dr. Denton onesies, and the tag line read, "Happy Holidays from the Lentz Dears." I ordered twenty-five cards, the minimum at Fotomat, and actually had some left over.

In 1988, I thought, *What the heck. I'll do one more year and that's it*. I photographed Jimmy and Jonathon in front of the fireplace, surrounded by holiday decorations, and the card read, "Warm wishes for the holiday." And then the next year, and the next, and the next. It was easy to come up with great cards for the first few years with simple props, sentimental themes, and cooperative kids. The cuteness factor was way off the charts.

This was the kinder, gentler Herman. My dark passenger hadn't yet jumped aboard for the ride. The next thing I knew, I was living for the rush. I'd discovered my drug of choice: creativity. I had a camera on my back, and each year, I had to take more chances to top the previous year's card. Thalia enabled my habit, unbeknownst to her. She had no idea that she was feeding the beast by designing props, coordinating outfits, and even posing in the pictures.

The reality was that I was lying to myself. I wasn't sending out the cards selflessly to wish our family and friends a happy holiday. If that were the case, I wouldn't have needed to come up with a new theme every year. Like everyone else, I could have found a cute picture of my kids and stuck it in an envelope. The hard truth is that my body craved the accolades and the adoration of the masses. I was a recognition junkie. Being complimented and celebrated for my comedic talents triggered a surge of endorphins through my body, putting me in a euphoric state.

I even strategized about when to send out my cards for maximum effect. I didn't want to send them out too early and appear needy, nor did I want to send them out too late and limit the amount of time people had to admire them and respond.

The day after I dropped the cards off at the post office, I would sit expectantly by the phone, waiting for a flurry of congratulatory phone calls. Like a market researcher, I documented the feedback I received. Comments like, "I liked last year's card better," or "I don't get it," would send me into a tailspin. At first, I mistakenly blamed myself and wallowed in self-pity. Eventually, I realized that the fault did not lie with me, but with the recipient's lack of imagination, vision, and sense of humor. I noticed trends, and if I got negative feedback from the same person two years in a row, they were dead to me. (Actually, I took them off my mailing list, which is the same thing.)

While I enjoyed the positive feedback, it was never enough. "Good job" or "Very funny" did not satiate me; I longed for more. I spent fucking months agonizing, countless hours and sleepless nights devoted to birthing each year's card. All I get in return is a smiley face emoji? The amount of thought, time, and effort that went into sending me a text message consisting of three letters, LOL, hardly seemed adequate.

And then there were the people who didn't acknowledge my cards at all. Maybe I was in denial, but I liked to believe that they were dumbstruck by total awe and couldn't comment because they were incapable of putting their adulation into words. It was the only reasonable explanation.

I hid my addiction for years. I couldn't wait for December to roll around so I could get my next fix, and I even found myself thinking about themes during the summer.

And then the worst happened: Jimmy and Jonathon refused to pose for any more pictures. Being a junkie, I tried, I lied, and I even bribed. They refused all of my offers. The kids were out; screw 'em, the ungrateful little bastards. There was no turning back for me, I was hopelessly hooked. With no other alternatives, I started photoshopping our dogs into my holiday pictures. I was becoming unhinged. The quality of my cards went to shit, and things got ugly. I was on the verge of losing everything I had worked so hard for over the years.

In 2007, I hit rock bottom. That year, I sent out a card that read, "Happy Holidays from Oy and Goy." I only share this story because my recovery requires me to face my demons. The concept was doomed from the start. The card featured Santa Claus and Tevye from *Fiddler on the Roof*, arguing on a roof next to the chimney. I photoshopped my two Yorkies' heads onto the men's bodies. Santa was shouting, "Chimney," and Tevye was yelling, "Roof! Roof!" What the fuck was I thinking?

Needless to say, there was no joy in Mudville—mighty Herman had struck out. The haters didn't hate, it was too easy. The silent majority thankfully remained silent. The close family and friends who remained discussed staging an intervention. That year, I realized I needed help, badly. I couldn't continue down the path I was on. I couldn't quit cold turkey, I'm way too weak willed. I had been hooked on cards for twenty-one years, and I had to find a way to wean myself off my addiction.

I decided that I'd send out Hallmark cards that were creative, witty, and would somewhat capture my essence. I went to a greeting card store in the mall and perused the prepackaged boxes of cards. Despite the depth and breadth of the collection, the pithy sayings and scenes depicting winter frolicking barely masked the antiseptic sterility of the selection. I picked out an innocuous set of cards, but I felt dead on the inside.

I was concerned about how people would react. I imagined their worried faces as they received that year's card: "Has Herman joined a cult?" "Did he suffer serious head trauma?" "Has Thalia finally broken him after all these years?"

One day, I had a stroke of luck. A coworker mentioned that her husband worked in an art studio. I started fantasizing about working with an artist. The possibilities were endless; the only limit was my imagination. *It wouldn't hurt just to talk*, I told myself.

She gave me the phone number for Avon Barksdale, their most creative artist. I kept his card in my wallet for a few days and resisted taking it out. Alas, I was battling addiction and suffering creativity withdrawals, so I succumbed to my urges and called.

Avon became artistic heroin. He took my exhaustive notes and stick figure drawings, blew my mind, and expanded my creative horizons. The first card he created for me wasn't expensive, and the rush was unbelievable. I was hooked. With total creative freedom, my imagination could run rampant. What a rush!

My mind was overwhelmed with ideas for themes and pictures. I listened to holiday songs around the clock, searching for that hidden phrase that would be the inspiration for the next card. I cruised the racks of greeting cards in the waiting rooms of car washes, looking for ideas.

The moment I finished one card, I would start on the next. The cycle was beginning to affect my daily life. My habit got so bad that I started working on multiple cards at a time, and I even had a secret stash of cards hidden in the house that I didn't want Thalia to know about. More than once, I found myself sitting in front of my computer in my underwear amidst the squalor and putrid stench of humorless writing, looking for the perfect pun in the middle of the night. I was constantly parched from mouthing the words to pathetic jokes over and over. I was fidgety and couldn't sit still, scratching myself as I searched for the right double entendre or clever word association. And then suddenly, I would lift my head to start writing a joke, but inevitably, I realized I had nothing. Every time, I slowly lowered my head and shook it side to side in sad resignation.

Avon owned me, and he knew it. First he started charging me for changes, then he started raising his fees. One year, after he finished a picture and knew I would be satisfied for a while, he asked if I wanted to experiment and try something new. I was scared but curious. He offered to paint a picture of my dogs. Skeptically, I thought, *What's next, my kids? A Lentz family portrait? A Lentz extended family portrait? How deep does this rabbit hole go?*

Designing holiday cards just didn't cut it anymore. My body craved more recognition. I started adding a letter to accompany the cards. It was just a few lines at first, to test the waters, but it quickly morphed into a full-blown narrative. Not only would I wow my audience with the artistic nuances of my card, but my comedic talents would dazzle them with the witty repartee in my letter.

My mental state deteriorated exponentially. Once a year was no longer cutting it for me; I needed a fix more frequently, so I launched a website in September 2018. On the first of every month, I posted a new story for my adoring fans. Minutes after posting it, I used the embedded analytics tools to track everyone who viewed my story and how many times they visited my site. As good as that high was, I hungered for more. I needed instant gratification, which led me to compete in storytelling competitions and read my stories at open mic nights sponsored by a local writing school.

I have accepted the fact that I am a recognition junkie. With the yearly holiday card, the monthly blog post, and the occasional open mic night, my habit is under control. I can finally be a functioning member of society again. It's not like I'm going to hit another rock bottom, hire an editor, and publish a book of my stories.

Oops.

The Summer of Herman

It was the summer of 1974. I had just turned nineteen and had gotten a job as a counselor at a sleepaway camp. I'd been a camper since the age of six and had worked as a waiter for the camp the previous summer, and it was finally time to culminate my camp experience as a counselor. Summer sleepaway camp is a Long Island Jewish tradition. After the school year ends in June, Jewish parents ship their children off to camp as quickly as possible and at an exorbitant cost, which they gladly pay. Camp ends minutes before the new school year begins in the fall.

The counselors arrived at the camp two days early to set everything up for the campers and get settled into their cabins. Since I had tenure after attending the camp for years, I was one of the first to select which group of campers I wanted. It was a coed camp, so I requested the seventeen-year-old girls. My request was heartlessly rejected. My second choice was the thirteen-year-old boys, who I thought would be a lot of fun. They're old enough for the sports to be competitive, but still young enough that they didn't have insolent attitudes like the older boys did. After all, what else could thirteen-year-old boys be into besides sports? I envisioned my days spent playing baseball, basketball, football, and tennis, and my nights spent over on the girls' side of the camp. It promised to be the summer of Herman.

I could just picture it: summer days driftin' away to those summer nights . . .

When the campers arrived, something seemed off. I chalked it up to new counselor jitters and got my kids all settled in. On the third night, my friend Mike and I staggered back to the cabin after a night of partying. We didn't want to wake our campers or let them know the condition we were in, so we snuck to our respective bunks.

Five to ten minutes later, one camper said, "Hey Mike, you awake?"

Mike didn't reply. He was already passed out.

Then the camper asked, "Herman, you awake?" I didn't respond, so the kid said, "Okay guys, it's cool."

What is going on? I wondered. The boys all pulled down their blankets, and I still couldn't make any sense of it. *They are just lying there. What the hell are they doing?*

And then.

Apparently, just before camp began, my campers discovered that they had the ability to reproduce, and they found great pleasure in practicing with themselves. My initial reaction was that boys will be boys. I remembered when I was thirteen and a friend got a porno movie. I stole five bucks from my mother's mahjong jar to pay for admission. Halfway through the movie, there was a knock on the door. It was the police. We all bolted out the back, planning to jump on our ten-speed Schwinn bicycles to make our getaway, but a cop car came screeching down the street and blocked our path.

We yelled, "Don't shoot! Don't shoot!" With our hands in the air, we walked back into the house, where the police officer took our names and phone numbers. Then he told us that they were going to call our parents and tell them what we were doing.

"Shoot! It's okay, go ahead and shoot!"

As I lay in my camp bunk that night, I remembered the joy I experienced when I first discovered this mode of self-actualization. But unlike these little perverts, I never made it into a group activity. As I discreetly pulled my blanket over my head and covered my ears with my pillow, the guys were screaming out girls' names and the names of their middle-school teachers. *Oh the horror! The horror!* I was buzzed, and those kids were really going at it. How long could they keep it up? It must have been a while, since they repeated a few of the names a third and fourth time.

Finally, *mercifully*, I fell asleep. The next morning, I recalled the debauchery of the previous evening and tried to make sense of it. My definition of group sex differed greatly from theirs, and I desperately hoped it was a one-time occurrence. I was freaked out. At breakfast, I hardly ate anything at all, but my campers attacked their meal ravenously. I told them we were scheduled to play baseball that morning. To my surprise, they moaned and groaned in protest.

"What do you mean you're not in the mood? It's a beautiful day, and we got Field A. It's a perfect day for baseball!"

One of the bolder boys said, "I think we'd all rather hang out in the cabin today."

"What the hell are you going to do in the cabin all morning?" I asked. But then I realized that their guns were all reloaded and they were raring to go. Unfortunately, this was not an isolated event; it was all they wanted to do. They'd hit the mother lode and their supply was limitless. They especially loved stormy days since they got to hang out in the bunk all day. Before long, they could have bent a steel bar with one hand, but they could hardly throw a baseball with the other.

This was not what I signed up for.

Every night, it was the same thing. "Hey Herman, you awake?"

"Yep, I'm wide awake. Not going to sleep, gonna be up all night. Not tired at all. Nope, nope, nope."

As the longest week of my life drew to a close, there was at least something to look forward to: the first coed social with the girls' camp was approaching. *Let's see what these little deviants do when they actually see a girl*, I thought. *Revenge is a dish best served cold.*

On the night of the dance, the girls were lined up on one side of the gymnasium, and the boys were on the other side. Center court was the demilitarized zone, which was not crossed the entire evening. My degenerates were running in circles beneath the basket, hitting each other, knocking each other's hats off, and making farting sounds. I couldn't be more pleased with how socially inept they were. The girls just looked at them in disgust. Since this was the first coed event of the summer, everyone had to introduce themselves. The boys went first; most of their voices cracked as they said their names.

Then it was the girls' turn. The first girl up was Mindy Rappaport. *Do I know a Mindy Rappaport? Where have I heard that name before?* Next was Fern Goldberg. *Hmm, that rings a bell*, I thought. As Beth something-stein said her name, I shrieked in gruesome recognition. *Oh, no! These are the names I've been hearing for the past week in the throes of pubescent ecstasy!*

I turned to Mike and said, "I don't want to sleep in the bunk tonight. It's going to be bad, man, real bad."

Things were not going the way I had imagined with my campers, but at least I had an active social life. I met a girl crazy for me. Let me tell you more. Her name was Sandy, she was seventeen, she had blue eyes and dirty blonde hair, and she was going into her senior year of high school. She may have appeared sweet and pure, but our nocturnal activities proved otherwise. Our summer nights made up for every disgusting moment with my shameless campers.

Then one day, little Randy Birnbaum approached me in tears. Despite the fact that he had recently celebrated his bar mitzvah and Jewish tradition considered him to be a man, Randy's biological clock hadn't gotten the memo. Despite how hard he tried, he couldn't successfully participate in the nighttime activities with his bunkmates. He wanted my advice. Had he been Catholic, I would have recommended the priesthood. That way, thirteen-year-old boys masturbating wouldn't have any effect on him.

And what about me? I wanted advice too! I hadn't signed up to play babysitter to a bunch of horny, pimple-faced idiots. My summer dreams were ripped at the seams. The entire camp knew what was going on. The camp slogan became, "If Herman's cabin is a-rockin', his campers are jerking off," which I thought was a very creative take on a classic.

I befriended little Randy, and while the rest of my campers were engaging in their depravity, Randy and I would play catch, shoot hoops, and kibitz. He was a good kid (i.e., he laughed at my stories) and I liked him.

A few weeks into the summer, Visiting Day was approaching, a time for parents to come up for the day to see their kids and meet the counselors. I panicked when I realized that they might ask how or what their sons were doing at camp. I mulled over a few potential responses beforehand:

"Well, at this rate, he will be blind by his next birthday."

"I guess he is really into moisturizing. That must be why he asked you to bring him an industrial-sized tub of Jergens lotion."

"The group enjoys arm wrestling, which explains the muscular tone of his one forearm."

"He's not really interested in team sports. He prefers playing with himself, I mean, by himself."

Visiting Day finally arrived, and the campers made a mad dash to greet their parents at the front gate. Interspersed with all the tanned, happy, healthy kids were my campers, who could be recognized by their pale and sallow complexions. They slowly made their way to the gate on legs that were practically atrophying. I said very little to the parents, with the exception of Mr. and Mrs. Birnbaum, and I survived Visiting Day unscathed.

A week later, the shit hit the fan. I thought I was the one that she wanted, but I found out our summer fling did not mean a thing. My group was the joke of the camp, and Sandy was teased for her relationship with the leader of the deviants. She was so embarrassed that she broke up with me. Guess mine was not the first heart broken. By that point, there were only a couple of weeks of camp left, so I figured that I could survive without her. *I'll just hang out with little Randy*, I thought. *I feel like I've become his mentor. He'll probably remember his favorite camp counselor for the rest of his life.* I felt really good about that.

But then one day, I caught up to Randy and suggested that we play some basketball.

His voice squeaked and cracked when he said, "I think I'm just going to hang out in the cabin for a while."

Alas, little Randy was little no more. He was all grown up and had become "RANDY!"

I found myself with no summer girlfriend, no mentee, and two long weeks left of camp. Well, if you can't beat 'em . . .

Is It Finished Yet?

There is a great novel by Irving Stone called, *The Agony and the Ecstasy*. No, it's not an erotic book about BDSM. It tells the story of the struggles between Michelangelo and Pope Julius II over the painting of the Sistine Chapel. Even though Michelangelo was a world-renowned sculptor, the pope commissioned (a.k.a. forced) Michelangelo to paint the ceiling of the Sistine Chapel. Michelangelo was a visionary and a perfectionist, so the job took a considerable amount of time, frustrating the pope to no end. Pope Julius constantly badgered Michelangelo: **"È finito ancora?"** (Is it finished yet?) and **"Quando sarà fatto?"** (When will it be done?). Perhaps the pope thought the ceiling only needed a bit of primer and a quick coat of paint. Instead, the end result was a masterpiece, widely regarded as one of the major artistic accomplishments of human civilization.

While Thalia is no Michelangelo and I am definitely no pope, she is a remarkably talented Renaissance woman. I literally only see things in black and white, but Thalia works with a full palette of colors and has an innate sense of style and vision. She can look at something incomplete or broken and see its potential. She can visualize what the outcome of her efforts will be. Maybe this is why she married me: she saw my potential. Unfortunately, I'm still a work in progress. As hard as she tries to mold me, I still don't remember to turn off the lights in the bathroom, and much to her annoyance, I still leave all the drawers open.

About fifteen years ago, she felt that Friday nights should be *Thalia Time*. I wondered how this was different from every other day of the week, which was also *Thalia Time*, but I knew better than to ask. On Fridays after dinner, she would relax in her Jacuzzi, watch HGTV, and enjoy a glass of wine, free from the stresses of work and the demands of her husband and kids.

I fully supported her wishes and truly believe that she deserved it. The only not-so-minor issue was that we didn't have a Jacuzzi, nor did we have a TV in our bathroom. While these impediments might deter mere mortals, Thalia saw them as an opportunity to spread her wings and be creative.

I have learned countless things from my marriage, but the two things that have served me best are:

1. When Thalia wants something, the vast majority of the time, she gets it. I can protest until I'm blue in the face, but ultimately, any resistance on my part is futile.

2. Any decision I make on decorating is always wrong, not just the majority of the time, but all the time. As a result, I have abdicated my decision-making rights. This works out well for both of us; I don't have to sweat the details and fear my

decision will be wrong, and she gets what she wants. Really, it's a win-win for Thalia.

Most would find the bathroom situation daunting, but for Thalia, it was a breeze. All that was required was to redesign our two upstairs bathrooms, which meant knocking down walls, reconfiguring the plumbing, redoing two showers, retiling both bathrooms, installing new cabinets, new countertops, new sinks, and new hardware, painting, updating the electric, and wiring for cable TV. A piece of cake! Fly Thalia fly!

Thalia's father was in the construction business, and when she told him what she wanted, he tried to dissuade her. He asked, "What do you need a Jamuzzi for?"

I know it's probably a tad insensitive of me to poke fun at his accent, but no matter how many times I corrected him, he still got it wrong. It made me smile each time.

He has obviously known Thalia longer than I have, so he knew very well that when she sets her mind to something, she will get it. He realized that he would have to help her install a Jamuzzi.

The first thing the co-general contractors, Thalia and her dad, did was to purchase a Jacuzzi. When it was delivered, instead of leaving it in the garage until we were ready to install it, Thalia decided that the delivery men should put it in our bedroom so we wouldn't have to deal with bringing it upstairs later. I was not involved in that decision, but I fully supported it until I bumped into the Jacuzzi every time I woke up in the middle of the night to go to the bathroom (which was a lot less frequently back then).

As anyone who has ever dealt with construction knows, nothing ever goes according to plan or finishes on time. Aside from the many unforeseen issues that pop up when you open walls, there are endless problems, including getting additional permits, inspection delays, contractors not showing up, workers not showing up, Contractor A taking so long that Contractor B can't start, Contractor B starting a job elsewhere and throwing the schedule completely to shit, things not being delivered on time (with the exception of the intrusive Jacuzzi), and the wrong items being delivered. Most days, it felt like nothing could go right.

Meanwhile, like Pope Julius, Thalia frequently asked each contractor, "Is it finished yet? When will it be done?" Not exactly known for her patience to begin with, she could only envision that first Friday night with the soothing jet streams of the Jacuzzi, the scented candles adorning the room, the lights dimmed, the wine chilled, and the TV playing her favorite show. The delays were killing her. I suffered too, arguably more. One night, on my way to the toilet, I bumped into the Jacuzzi and broke a toe. It was only my pinkie toe, but genetically, I have a nonexistent pain threshold, and between sobs, I cursed her and the fucking Jamuzzi while demanding that she drive me to the ER. She just rolled over and went back to sleep.

After months of construction and grueling physical therapy for my toe, everything was finally finished. The first Friday of *Thalia Time* was upon us. She was so excited. The scene was set, she entered her new haven, and all was right with the world. For about ten minutes. She came out of the bathroom to announce that the water in the Jacuzzi was lukewarm at best.

Well, it turned out our accomplished co-GCs had purchased a seventy-five-gallon Jamuzzi, which could not be filled by the fifty-gallon water heater we have in our basement. (Why would I even consider giving up my right to abstain from decision-making? I can't be blamed when things go wrong!)

One might think that the solution would be as simple as buying a larger water heater. It's not so easy. Our house only has a quarter basement, and the rest is a crawl space. There isn't much room down there for a larger tank. Should we get another fifty-gallon water heater to run in tandem? Or should we purchase a one-hundred-gallon water heater, which would require reconfiguring the basement?

I was annoyed. I told Thalia how pissed I was at the co-GCs and recommended that we either fire or sue them. At a minimum, I certainly wouldn't pay them. It wasn't the first time, nor the last, that Thalia realized that I need a lot more work than she thought when she married me. She tactfully ignored my comment.

Once again, a parade of tradespeople were working in my house, making a big mess, and spending my money. And once again, Thalia asked, "Is it finished yet? When will it be done?"

Finally, after another two agonizing months, everything was completed. *Thalia Time 2.0* was upon us. The scene was set once again: one hundred gallons of hot water, candles, dimmed lights, chilled wine, TV. Perfection. After everything she had been through, she deserved and needed the relaxation. She entered the bathroom for Thalia's Moment of Zen.

After only ten minutes, she came out of the bathroom, complaining that it was too hot in there, that she couldn't breathe. Nobody had considered the fact that since the bathroom is in the center of the house, it doesn't have a window. Seventy-five gallons of hot water can fog up a room pretty quickly.

She hasn't used the tub since. We were stuck with the conundrum of what to do with a seventy-five-gallon Jamuzzi that no one will use. Do we turn it into a planter for succulents? An indoor koi pond? A spa for our two Yorkies?

Well, after thirty-two years of living in our house, Thalia has flown with the eagles: three major extensions and multiple renovations and upgrades. It is physically and logistically impossible to do anything else to the house, so Thalia has decided it is time to move. She already has her first binder prepared with ideas, sketches, floor plans, surveys, pictures, and things to buy for the new house. She can't wait to get started.

All I can think is, "Is it finished yet? When will it be done?"

Saga of an Aging Gunslinger

I don't tell jokes. I am a storyteller, a weaver of yarns. I exaggerate, I enhance, but I do not tell jokes. And I must admit, I prefer using my own material. When someone tells me a joke, I have to fake a smile, offer an appropriate chuckle or head nod, and maybe throw in a back-slap at the end. Yuk yuk yuk.

In an exception to my general rule about using other people's material, I do enjoy the one-liners that work their way into our daily lexicon. For example, if I were to say, "Hello, Newman," people catch the reference right away, remembering the underlining animosity between Jerry Seinfeld and Newman. If they aren't familiar with the quote, they're not worth having a conversation with, so I just walk away. One of my favorite lines is from the classic Henny Youngman joke about a cat on the roof.

A man left his cat with his brother while he went on vacation for a week. When he came back, he called his brother to see when he could pick the cat up. The brother hesitated, then said, "I'm so sorry, but while you were away, the cat died."

The man was very upset and yelled, "You know, you could have broken the news to me better than that. When I called, you could have said that the cat was on the roof and wouldn't come down. Then when I called the next day, you could have said that he had fallen off and the vet was working on patching him up. Then when I called the third day, you could have said he passed away."

The brother thought about it and apologized.

"So, how's Mom?" asked the man.

"She's on the roof and won't come down."

Brilliance, sheer brilliance. Back in the day, "Mom is on the roof" or "The cat is on the roof" became part of the vernacular. I really try to avoid using other people's material, but I love that line and would interject it whenever possible.

As everyone who knows me can attest, I pride myself on having a great head of hair and a rapier-like wit. I take special pride in my lightning-quick speed and my ability to never miss an opportunity for a witticism. Well, like the aging gunslinger in the old westerns, whose razor-sharp reflexes have slowed a notch, I recently missed an opportunity. It was a moment I would have pounced on in my younger days, a moment that bards would have sung ballads about.

Corey, our twelve-year-old Yorkie, was diagnosed with a cancerous tumor. It's not the funniest premise but stick with me. Our options were to start chemotherapy, schedule an operation to remove the tumor, or put him down when his health got really bad. I refused to subject our beloved senior dog to chemo, and we knew he wouldn't survive a surgery, so we opted to make him as comfortable as we could and wait until the time was right to say goodbye.

Corey had a good life and was a sweet little dog. His major problem was incontinence. He peed in the house all the time, and it eventually got so bad that we put diapers on him. As if owning a Yorkie wasn't emasculating enough, having one in a diaper was priceless. One of his diapers had a plaid pattern on it, so I would tell people that he is a Yorkshire terrier and the design is a replica of his family crest. I usually got blank stares in return, but I thought it was funny and kept telling the joke. (So much for a rapier-like wit.)

One evening, when it was time for his nightly walk, I called for Corey and he didn't respond. After twelve years, I foolishly thought he would become Lassie and obey a command. "Timmy slipped on pee and fell down the well? Good boy, Corey!" What the hell was I thinking?

I searched the house for him and found him lying under my desk. He had passed away in his sleep. I was sad, but I knew I wouldn't have had the heart to put him down, nor did I want to see him suffer. It was really a blessing that he went so peacefully.

Thalia was working late in the city that night and was planning to catch a later train. I faced a dilemma: should I wait until she gets home to break the news, or should I call her at work and let her decide whether I should take the body to the animal hospital or wait until she gets home to say her goodbyes? I decided to call and let her decide.

When she answered the phone, I said, "Thalia, Corey's dead." She responded with unintelligible sobbing noises, but eventually requested that I remove his body before she got home. As I drove to the animal hospital, I replayed the scene in my mind. Had I handled it tactfully and compassionately? Should I have done something different? Then I let out a deep moan, shook my head, and sighed. I'd missed a golden opportunity.

When I called her, I should have said, "Thalia, Corey is on the roof."

Upon reflection, I was shaken. I had the perfect set up and I blew it. Had my lightsaber-like wit started to dim? If my reflexes were starting to show signs of age, I feared that all the people who I have snarked in the past would come gunning for me. Deep down, I always knew there would come a day when my past would catch up with me, but at that moment, while taking Corey to his final resting, I made a vow. *Today is not the day, and I will never miss an opportunity like that again*, I thought.

A few months later, I got a call from my cousin in California, telling me that my uncle had passed away. He wanted me to notify the family.

Hmmm . . .

Where the Sun Don't Shine

In the days before the internet and myriad dating websites, one way to meet people was to go on a Club Med vacation. Each Club Med location had its own unique reputation and target audience. As I leafed through the brochure, I turned the page as soon as I saw the word "family." I wasn't looking to spend my vacation around a bunch of screaming kids. Finally, I found the two words I had been searching for: "nude beach." And if that weren't enough, the word hedonism appeared in the copy. I was sold. I quickly called a travel agent and booked a vacation to Buccaneer's Creek in Martinique.

As I was counting down the days, hours, and minutes until my trip, my mantra was, "nude beach." I was subsisting on a rabbit-like diet of greens, but with each unsatisfying bite, I pictured the splendors of a nude beach to squash any cravings I had for a bacon cheeseburger, or G-d forgive me, veal parmigiana. When I thought my body was spent and had nothing left, I pushed myself to do one more push-up, one more sit-up, grunting, "nude beach."

Finally, pounds lighter and a lot tighter, the big day had arrived. I was at JFK airport, ready to board a charter flight to Martinique. When the plane landed in the French Caribbean, a Club Med bus picked us up to transport us to the resort. The bus was awkwardly silent, except for the soft murmur of all the men chanting "nude beach" under their breath. The closer we got to the resort, the louder the chanting grew. Like the running of the bulls in Pamplona, there was an all-male dash to the nude beach the moment we stepped off the bus. We didn't check in and abandoned our luggage in the lobby. We were like lemmings running to the sea. Luckily, no one was trampled as men stumbled and fell, littering the path to the nude beach with articles of clothing they shed along the way.

Sure enough, there were naked women on the beach. Some should have followed my pre-vacation regimen of no carbs, but for the most part, my fantasy became a reality. There was only one problem: I had never pictured other men on the beach. The clusters of these men were spoiling my view. Many of them looked like they came out of a Russian bath house, they also should have followed my pre-vacation regimen, creating an appalling panorama of sweat, body hair, and girth.

After choosing a scenic spot, I stretched out on the sand. Just as I was getting comfortable, I scanned the horizon, and then my body betrayed me. I may have been lighter and tighter, but my body was responding to the sensual stimuli around me. Like a divining rod finding water, if I needed to search the heavens and find the North Star, all I had to do was look down.

To hide my situation, I quickly jogged into the ocean. As I stood there with the water up to my waist, I noticed a lot of the guys from the flight in a similar position. Just when I thought it was safe to return to the beach, each time I caught sight of what was on the shore, my physiology prevailed and I had to head back into the water. I finally made it out as dusk settled in.

With all of the time I spend in the water, my lower body looked like a Sunmaid raisin.

After a day or two, just like Darwin's theory of evolution, I finally made it out of the water and onto dry land. I also proved the Costanza hypothesis to be true: long-term exposure to water will cause the phenomenon known as "Organus Smallus," or in layman's terms, "shrinkage."

So here I am, on the beach, full frontal Herman, unencumbered by any undergarments. However, being unaccustomed to this type of freedom, while trying to act inconspicuous, I must have looked like a fish out of water, flapping around in every direction trying to find a comfortable position.

Certain parts of my body have never been exposed to direct sunlight, but since applying lotion to that area is kind of creepy (both in the application process and the appearance of the area after you're all lathered up), I foolishly did not take any precautions. Back at the hotel room that night, when I was getting ready to shower, I noticed that my groin area looked like the core of the Chernobyl nuclear reactor as it was melting down. I had fallen victim to the dangers of a high UV index. I was sunburned. Badly.

Every man can attest to the pain and agony of blue balls. Well, that's nothing compared to the agony of sunburned genitals, or "Lobster Balls." (I wonder if I can copyright that?) Applying aloe to soothe the pain was akin to giving a junkie control of the morphine drip. I was slathering aloe all over, I guess I was applying it a tad to generously as I left a permanent stain on the chair and bed sheets. I even slipped off the toilet bowl seat. But I could not relieve the pain I was in.

With great distress, I made my way to the infirmary. I found myself standing at the end of a long queue of men. The line was awkwardly silent, except for the soft murmur of all the men chanting "owwww" under their breath. It seemed as though they'd all made the same mistake I had.

My delusions of sexual grander gone, as the only action I got that week was with the Club Med Doctor, Dr. Mengele. There was no small talk or foreplay, as he not so gingerly examined the extent of my agony. I thought, *Please G-d, don't let it blister and peel.*

I don't know what happened on the rest of the island at night, during the day, behind closed doors, in the pool, on the beach, or behind a bush, nor did I care. My most sensitive area had become even more sensitive. The only place I wanted to put it was into a bucket of ice water. Hedonism, my ass. I just wanted to pee without pain.

Needless to say, that vacation was anything but indulgent or pleasurable. I had learned a valuable lesson. The following year, as I perused the Club Med brochure again, I looked to see if they had a club in Alaska or the Arctic Circle, either of which would be lovely to visit in the winter. *Won't have to worry about Lobster Balls© in the Arctic*, I thought. But then a more gruesome thought crossed my mind. *Oh shit, its fucking cold. Frostbite can lead to Ballsicles©. Peeling is nothing compared to it snapping off!*

Instead, I chose Paradise Island, a "fun spot for singles." I was single, I wanted to have fun, and I was fully healed. What could possibly happen?

Well on the second day, I met my future wife, causing the phenomenon known as "Jewish Husbandinitis" or in layman's terms, "no balls".

The B-Word

Thalia and I rarely fight. This isn't because I consider myself to be a lover and not a fighter, but because even when I'm in the right, I lose the argument for reasons with no foundation in logic or justice.

Several years ago, however, we got into a big argument about the depth and breadth of Jimmy and Jen's wedding guest list. Thalia has a good heart, while I am heartless. She doesn't want to hurt anyone's feelings, while I might tend to be a tad sarcastic. She likes people, while I am disliked by the general public, perhaps because of my snarkiness. Needless to say, we are very different.

Thalia comes from a Greek family. I could have included the word "big" in front of "Greek family," but that would have been redundant. Every Greek family is big. First cousins, second cousins, cousins countlessly removed, godparents, godchildren, relatives of godparents and godchildren, in-laws and their entire clan, and people from the same village or island in the old country—they are all treated as members of the nuclear family. On the other hand, I am a happily self-imposed orphan.

When it was time to send wedding invitations, Thalia emailed me her version of the guest list. It was in a zip file since it was too large to send as an attachment. *This can't be good*, I thought. Not only was the list impossibly, comically long, but since the majority of invitees were of Greek descent, each full name had about eighty-three letters. I didn't recognize a lot of the names, and I couldn't even pronounce the vast majority of them. The vowel-to-consonant ratio in Greek names is close to 50:50. When Thalia became a Lentz, she lost four vowels in her last name. I wondered if they could even syndicate *Wheel of Fortune* in Greece. Do the contestants spin for vowels and pay for letters? The puzzle board would have to be at least twice the size of the American version.

I told her she had to cut the wedding list. She defended everyone's right to attend, like she was holding Schindler's List. She refused to remove a single name.

It wasn't only the guest list that caused us to butt heads. There were so many Thalia extras, or "little touches" as she would call them, that she always throws in to make things different and special. Little touches come with big price tags. For example, after James and Jenny said their vows, Thalia decided that she wanted to add a touch of elegance by releasing one hundred butterflies to swirl around the bride and groom as they stood at the altar. Yep, they sell freeze-dried butterflies that can be thawed out before the ceremony.

When Thalia told me she wanted to do this, I thought it was a ridiculous idea. Why not doves, skywriting, or skydivers? Maybe flying Elvis skydivers! Then I thought about a movie from the '70s,

Butterflies are Free. Not only are frozen butterflies not free, but they come at an exorbitant cost. I guess a wedding on the beach at sunset, the waves lapping at the shore, palm trees rustling in the wind was not special enough—we needed Painted Lady butterflies. It was a spectacular twelve seconds, but the cost per second was hardly justifiable.

Thalia also heard about an artist who painted a portrait of the reception while it was going on. She simply had to have him. I found it a tad redundant; we had both a photographer and a videographer covering the event. Would the photographer take a picture of the artist painting the portrait? Would the videographer film a time-lapse documentary of the artist as he practiced his craft? Would the artist include the photographer and videographer in the painting? Would my American Express card be able to cover them all?

And of course we needed wedding favors. Not the standard-fare trinkets sitting lamely on a banquet table that guests ignore while searching for their valet ticket. No, no, no, that just wouldn't do. The favors had to be Thalia-ized. She ordered 252 succulents, along with 252 glass containers to put them in. She also needed twenty pounds of MiracleGro succulent soil to put into the 252 glass containers so the 252 succulents would flourish. Naturally, we had to order ribbons with James & Jenny's names and the wedding date on them to tie around the containers. Each one had to be planted by hand and the ribbon tied on, and then the whole thing had to be schlepped to the venue.

With the stress of wedding planning piling up, we had a semi-heated discussion over the guest list and the rising cost of all the extras.

A few weeks later, Thalia said she was really upset with me. Being the understanding, compassionate person that I am, I said,

"Okay, sweetheart. If you're upset about something, let's talk about it." I usually like to know what I need to apologize for before I actually apologize.

She said, "I'm upset with the language you used with me."

"Thalia, I have no idea what you're talking about."

She stood her ground. "When we talked about the wedding earlier this month, you used the worst possible word with me."

I was still clueless.

"You have to promise never to use that word with me again."

I was totally lost. "Sweetheart, what word are you talking about?"

"The B-word."

The B-word? *Did I call her a bitch? That's not like me.* My mind was racing. While I couldn't imagine that I ever would have called Thalia a bitch, it's not like I used the C-word.

Unable to recall doing such a thing, I said, "Thalia, the B-word? Are you sure?"

She responded, "Yes, I was very hurt. It's the worst possible word you can say to me. Please promise me that you will never use it again.

"Thalia, I am truly sorry I called you a bitch. It was insensitive and wrong. I promise I will never call you a bitch again."

She looked shocked. "You didn't call me a bitch! I said you used the B-word, the worst word you can say to me: BUDGET."

Tradition

I first noticed Jill during Rosh Hashanah services at temple. It was my first semester at Boston University, and I had come home for the Jewish holidays. On Rosh Hashanah, we believe that G-d opens the Book of Life to chronicle the fates of the wicked, the righteous, and the intermediate class. He records the names of the righteous and condemns the wicked to the Book of the Dead, and the rest of us spend the next ten days reflecting and repenting. Then, on Yom Kippur, the book is sealed, and your fate is determined. As usual, I had a lot to atone for.

Jill was in the choir, and she caught my eye right away. I should have been asking G-d for forgiveness of my sins and transgressions from the past year and hopefully putting in a good word for the upcoming year, but instead, I was fixated on the clinginess of her choir robe. She wasn't my usual type, which, to the annoyance of my parents, included any female of non-Jewish persuasion. However, with her long, curly, brown hair, wide smile, and curvy physique, I felt a primal attraction. I thought, *My G-d, what has become of me? It's like I'm being pulled by centuries of Jewish breeding*. The attraction was downright Talmudic. I found myself humming the song "Tradition" from *Fiddler on the Roof*, and like Tevye, I felt compelled to throw my hands up in the air and start dancing.

My thoughts may have been inappropriate, but if viewed within a biblical context, I was simply homing in on the sections of the Bible that featured a lot of begetting. I wanted to follow in the traditions of the patriarchs. Because of my obsession with Jill, I spent more time in the synagogue than usual, and less time outside with my friends, smoking cigarettes. While reading the Torah, bowing, humming along to the Hebrew songs, and genuflecting, I was thinking about our future together and asking the questions any prospective Jewish groom would ask himself. Which country club should host our wedding? Did her father own a successful business I could join, and hopefully have no sons to share it with? Did her grandparents have money?

I knew I needed to become a better person for my betrothed, so I had to atone for all my sins and start the new year with a clean slate. During the high holidays, we recite the "Al Chet" prayer, which is a confession of our sins. While the prayer comprises forty-four potential sins, I tended to abuse some significantly more than others. For example, I had to ask forgiveness for:

- The mistakes I committed with endless babbling.
  (Has G-d read my stories?)

- The mistakes I committed through negative speech.
  (Negative speech is my native tongue.)

- The mistakes I committed willfully and unintentionally. (Okay, I can understand willfully, but unintentionally? Come on!)

Jews consider ourselves to be the "Chosen People," but why? For being supposedly holy people, we sure do have to atone for quite a lot of sinning.

My strategy was to space out my sins slowly throughout the year. It was a bit like saving money in the bank for a rainy day, and if I hadn't hit my yearly sin quota by Rosh Hashanah, it was a bad time to fuck with me. The extra sins were burning a hole in my pocket. I decided that it was smartest to wait until after the holidays to ask Jill out, when my slate was clean.

At first, I didn't think anything of it when Jill said I could pick her up after sundown on Saturday night. But then I pieced it together: she was in the temple choir, she couldn't go out until after the Sabbath was over—Jill was a Conservative Jew. Something wasn't kosher, and apparently, it was me. I am a Reformed Jew and practice Judaism Lite (same great traditions, less guilt). For my future bride, however, I was willing to make sacrifices, with the exception of cheeseburgers and bacon, of course.

What I didn't know was that she was the cantor's daughter! The cantor is an important part of the synagogue, leading the congregation in song and prayer from the altar, alongside the rabbi. He also helps the twelve-year-old Jewish boys prepare for their bar mitzvahs, teaching them how to sing in Hebrew from the Torah in front of their family, friends, and the entire congregation. (This is the price we have to pay to be the star in the Cecil B. DeMille production of the bar mitzvah celebration that follows.)

Unfortunately, I had a bad history with my congregation's cantor. I had been a terrible Hebrew school student. There was a hobby shop across the street from the temple that sold used copies of *Mad Magazine*; the money that I was supposed to donate to charity to plant trees in Israel went toward my reading collection instead. Hopefully, the trees were going to be planted in the Palestinian section so I wouldn't have to feel as bad.

Since I spent too much time with Alfred E. Neuman, I was ill prepared to sing what turned out to be fifty-nine lines of Hebrew. Needless to say, the cantor was not pleased with my total lack of proficiency, as I couldn't read, write, or speak the language. After my lousy performance, I was in no position to ask out his daughter, but I was determined to win her hand anyway. Going into her family business was certainly out of the question. Oy! Despite being at a disadvantage, I wanted to make a good impression. As a graduate of the Eddie Haskell School of Suck-Ups, I was skilled at charming the parents of my victims, I mean, dates.

On the night of my first date with Jill, I put on my winningest smile. "How nice to meet you, Mrs. Pearlmutter. What a lovely home you have. I know I'm a week late, but I hope you have a very happy and healthy new year."

"How nice. Jill tells me you belong to our temple. You must know my husband. Izzy, come downstairs and meet Jill's little friend."

Like Charlton Heston in *The Ten Commandments*, Cantor Ishak Pearlmutter regally descended the staircase wearing a robe and slippers and carrying a Bible. I instantly felt like Edward G. Robinson dancing around the golden calf. *This can't be good*, I thought.

"Izzy, do you remember Herman Lentz? He's a nice Jewish boy and a member of our congregation. He's taking out our Jill tonight."

Cantor Pearlmutter said, "Herman Lentz, Herman Lentz... your Jewish name wouldn't be Chaim, would it?"

Oy vey, he remembers me. Maybe he doesn't remember what a pain in the ass I was.

"Happy and healthy new year, Cantor Pearlmutter. How good to see you again! I really enjoyed the Rosh Hashanah and Yom Kippur services this year; they were some of your best."

He wasn't buying any of my schmaltz. He said, "So, what are you planning on doing with your life, Chaim?"

As much as I hate my name, Chaim is worse. I used to ask him to call me by my Judeo-Christian name instead, which of course he refused to do. Our battles had been of biblical proportion. For example, I didn't want to wear a yarmulke indoors, as I'd read in Ann Landers column that it was rude to wear a hat in the house. Fortunately, when he was in the yeshiva studying to become a cantor, he hadn't minored in circumcision and become a mohel as well. If he had, I probably would have sounded like Barry Gibb and sung my fifty-nine lines of Hebrew in a high falsetto.

"I'm going to Boston University as an accounting major, sir."

He shook his head sadly. "Not pre-med? My condolences to your parents."

Apparently he remembered everything. It was hopeless. The *Titanic* had hit the iceberg and was going down fast.

"I don't recall seeing you in temple much since your bar mitzvah, Chaim."

I thought, *You didn't see me in temple much before my bar mitzvah, either, Izzy.* Up against the ropes, swaying side to side and front to back, I looked like a Hasidic Jew in the midst of morning prayer.

"Chaim, tonight you are taking out my angel, the joy of my life, my precious Jill Amy Pearlmutter. You had better behave yourself." Just then it hit me: I was taking out the cantor's little princess, **J**ill **A**my **P**earlmutter, a true JAP. I knew in that moment that Jill and I were not destined to end up together. We wouldn't have any little Jews or Jewesses. In fact, our first date was probably going to be our last.

Despondent, my thoughts drifted back to my high school girl-friend, Colleen. Colleen was not Jewish and my parents hated her, both points that worked in her favor. Although her parents admitted the many positives of having a Jewish son-in-law, they hated me too. She was Irish and had a beautiful smattering of freckles across her cheeks; she had a Catholic schoolgirl, Ivory Snow beauty about her. When she wore a pleated skirt and sweater, I couldn't control myself. Had she also been a cheerleader, the ultimate prize for a Long Island Jew, I would have proposed to her.

Cantor Pearlmutter and Colleen's father were diametrically opposed, as the cantor epitomized the Jewish religion and Colleen's father hated the Jews. Despite their fundamental differences, they had two things in common. First, neither of them liked me. Second, they both refused to use my Judeo-Christian name, and the names they used instead sounded alike: the cantor called me Chaim and Colleen's father called me Hymen.

I knew that Colleen's father's comments, taunts, and his insistence on mangling my name were deliberate attempts to bother me, to break Hymen. The irony was that Colleen and I dated for over a year and had a lot of fun together. As it turned out, I was not the Hymen that was broken.

Screw You, Mr. Miyagi

When my boys were born, I knew that I didn't have any athletic prowess to pass on to them. So, when Jimmy and Jonathon were young, I started developing their senses of humor. They majored in sarcasm and minored in obnoxious. Their training was covert and had to be done without the knowledge of TTG (Thalia the Good), who would have preferred that I used my powers for good instead of evil. I was subjected to many a lecture when she caught us.

But it was all worth it. When Jimmy and Jon were about ten years old, the fruits of my labor were coming to fruition. Whenever we watched a TV show, just as the hero was surrounded by bad guys with their guns pointed at him and no possible way out, the program would break to commercial. I always said something like, "There is no way the hero is going to survive. He'll get killed. This is how the series ends!" Of course, the hero miraculously escaped every time, and good prevailed over evil in the end.

Once, Jimmy and Jonathon were watching *Free Willy* with their cousins, Billy and Stephen. The movie was coming to its climax. Willy the whale was trapped in an inlet, nets and breakwater preventing him from escaping into the ocean. The evil whalers were homing in on him and the tension was coming to a crescendo.

Just then, Jimmy paused the DVD and said, "Willy dies. He doesn't make it over the wall and the whalers get him."

I was bursting with pride. I couldn't have been prouder of my son.

Stephen, the youngest cousin, ran from the room, crying and screaming to his mother that Willy died. I knew I would get an earful from TTG, but it was worth it.

Billy said, "Wait, I've seen this movie before. Willy jumps over the wall and escapes to the ocean."

Quick-witted like his old man, Jonathon said, "They changed the ending for the DVD."

I was wrong. I could be prouder.

While I was extremely sarcastic as a kid (and some say I still am to this day), I was smart enough to choose my moments wisely, since I bruise easily. My only defense, which was not at all effective, was to use Jew-Jitsue, where you threaten to sue your adversary for everything they own. As the boys grew, I realized that teaching them to be sarcastic was not enough. They needed more, so I signed them up for karate lessons. If they were going to be snarky, they'd better learn how to defend themselves.

Jimmy and Jonathon became the first Lentzes to learn how to fight. Throughout history, the Lentzes have been terrorized by Egyptians, Mesopotamians, Phoenicians, and Romans. In modern times, even the Greeks have taken a swing or two. I was determined that the vicious cycle would end with my sons.

I had no idea what I was signing up for in terms of time or financial commitment. Screw you, Mr. Miyagi and your wax on, wax off nonsense. Three times a week for four years, the cost really added up. In addition to the monthly fees, every time they were up for a promotion, they had to take a test for a not-so-nominal charge. Being colorblind, I never knew how many shades of green, blue, or brown there are until I had to pay for a rainbow of colored belts. Tack on the expense of sparring equipment and tournament registration fees, and I was quickly going broke. I wasn't sure about his karate prowess, but I knew that this insensitive sensei was a black belt in billing.

Jimmy and Jonathon stuck with it, and before long, they both became proficient. Jimmy was very strong and had a bad temper. I lived in fear that I would get a call from his school. "Mr. Lentz, your son has just taken out the entire sixth grade."

Sure enough, one day I did receive a call. Jimmy had been involved in an "incident," and I was summoned to the principal's office. As I drove to the school, I feared that I would discover the schoolyard littered with broken children, moaning in agony. I pictured the scene: Jimmy is executing his best skills—roundhouse kicks, karate chops, elbow strikes, arm-bar holds—as the circle of kids closes in around him. With no way out, Jimmy is ready to concede defeat. Just then, Jonathon flies in to his brother's defense, does a double flip off a picnic table into the center of the circle, and stands back-to-back with Jimmy. In a dazzling display of martial arts prowess, they decimate all of their rivals. I thought of every bully who ever picked on me when I was growing up, and while I knew it was irrational, I could only hope that it was their child who was mangled that day.

I gathered myself as I pulled into the school parking lot. I was relieved that there were no ambulances or SWAT teams in riot gear preparing to storm the school. When I walked into the principal's office, I saw Jimmy sitting with his head hung. He mumbled, "Hey, Dad."

I looked him over, but I didn't see any marks or blemishes. I thought, *Yes! Jimmy won!* I had to fight the urge to high five him and do some strutting. I was a very proud dad.

"Mr. Lentz, James was involved in an altercation during lunch."

Sitting next to Jimmy was his adversary, but surprisingly, he wasn't scarred with marks or blemishes either. He was a rotund boy with glasses and thick, curly hair. I nodded to him and said, "Helloooo, Newman."

He grimaced at me.

"What exactly happened today, Principal Skinner?"

"Mr. Lentz, James was cruelly teasing Newman in front of everyone. Your son made him cry."

My bad, I thought. *I should probably update my sarcasm curriculum to include an ethics module.*

The principal continued. "Newman then punched James."

"Excuse me, Principal Skinner. While Jimmy certainly didn't learn this type of behavior at home and I don't condone teasing, it sounds to me like he didn't throw the first punch to start the fight."

"It gets worse, Mr. Lentz."

I braced myself for what would come next. Jimmy had been preparing for this moment three times a week for the past four years. Time probably slowed down, and Jimmy's instincts and training had taken over. I imagined that he put on an impressive exhibition, culminating with him sweeping Newman's leg.

"Sir, in front of the entire lunchroom, James pulled down Newman's pants."

"Are you saying that after he was physically assaulted, all Jimmy did was *pants* Newman?" *He can't be serious*, I thought. *This is kind of funny.* "Principal Skinner, don't you think that Jimmy actually behaved in a Gandhi like, nonviolent way to defuse the situation? At worst, he embarrassed Newman, and isn't that better than hitting him? I fail to see the problem here."

"Not only did James pants him, but he pulled down his underwear also!"

Jimmy had achieved the rare Pants Plus, and although that was going a tad too far, it does take a fairly high degree of manual dexterity to get the underwear. I wondered if Newman had been wearing boxers or tighty-whities. Tighty-whities would probably be more difficult, and boxer briefs would be nearly impossible. Again, I had to fight the urge to high five Jimmy.

Jimmy had to serve a two-day suspension and write a letter of apology to Newman, but I was proud of his restraint, so I took him to Dairy Queen on the way home. Needless to say, karate lessons officially ended that afternoon. I could have taught him everything he needed to know in a single afternoon and saved myself all that time and money.

Pants on, pants off.

Not My Finest Moment

Despite my snarky exterior, I like to think of myself as a good person, though my f1amily, friends, coworkers, casual acquaintances, and the general public may disagree. Am I perfect? No. Can I do appalling things? Unfortunately, yes. I would prefer to be judged for being a loving husband, a loyal friend, and a doting father, and not for the times my rapier-like wit slices through the funny bone and lacerates the psyche.

Of all my roles, I am most proud of being a doting father. When Jimmy and Jonathon were young, they played baseball and soccer, and eventually, they became ice hockey junkies. My weekends were consumed cheering them on at hockey matches, driving them to their hockey clubs, and supporting them on their high school hockey team. I loved every moment.

When the boys went off to college, there was a void in my life. I had nothing to do on the weekends. I had no hobbies. I continued to go to the high school and club games, but that started to get weird. I was concerned about being picked up on Megan's Law charges. With nothing to fill my time, I moped around the house. I got so desperate that I even contemplated going shopping with Thalia on the weekends, an endeavor that probably would have led to the end of our marriage.

So, at the advanced age of fifty-one, I started playing golf. ("Playing" is an extremely generous description of what I was doing.) I tend to be very hard on myself and sucking at anything pains me terribly. Since I really sucked at golf, I signed myself up for lessons. The instructor did the best he could to teach me the fundamentals of the game, but there was only so much he could do. I later learned that he was a recovering alcoholic, and I think he took up drinking again after working with me.

My first time on the golf course was at a Charles Schwab outing. I was extremely nervous to meet the other players in my foursome, so after shaking hands and introducing myself, I thought I'd break the ice.

I said, "I wanted to let you know that I have a mild case of Tourette's Syndrome, so I might be cursing on the golf course today."

They were very understanding, and all chimed in with assurances. "Oh, that's all right. Don't worry about it!"

It was then I confessed that I don't have Tourette's, that it was my first time on a golf course, and I was just very nervous. We all laughed, patted each other on the back, and had a lovely day. As expected, I sucked and there were many swears.

Yes, I know that making a joke about a terrible disease is deplorable. It's not something that I'm proud of, but unfortunately, my history of sensitivity is not stellar. When I was younger, I broke up with a girlfriend after a heated argument. Once, in the throes of passion, her arms and legs had started jerking, her body stiffened, and she nearly lost consciousness. The cause was obvious to me, but I wanted to hear her accolades for my sexual prowess, so I felt compelled to ask her if it was good for her also. She called me a fucker and told me that she was having a seizure. I begged to differ and broke up with her as I was considering a career in porn.

I tried to be more sensitive after the seizure incident, but I didn't always succeed. When my son was twenty-one, he was diagnosed with type 1 diabetes. Thalia and I wanted to learn as much as we could about the disease, so we attended the Juvenile Diabetes Research Foundation's annual gala fundraiser. The night was eventful and featured dinner, dancing, and keynote speakers discussing the progress being made on the race for a cure. At the end of the evening, they asked us to fill out a survey form about the event and hand it in before we left. All I wrote was, "The dessert sucked." Thalia was not amused.

Over the years, my golf skills have improved, not dramatically, but I have my moments. Eventually, I felt comfortable enough to walk onto a course and play with three strangers. As an icebreaker, I would occasionally use the Tourette's line. The other players would always laugh, then we'd all pat each other on the back and tee off.

One fateful day, I used the line as always. I braced myself for the feel-good camaraderie, but instead of patting me on the back, one of the guys put a consoling arm around my shoulder, squeezed it a little, and said, "That's all right. A member of my family has Tourette's. There's nothing to be ashamed of."

Oh no! No, no, no! Me and my big mouth.

I wasn't sure what to do. Should I admit that it was a joke and look like the biggest asshole in the continental United States? Or should I start indiscriminately screaming "motherfucker" and twitching? I considered my options. A typical round of golf takes about four hours, so if I carried on with the charade, I would have to determine how to space out my outbursts. Every hole? Every other hole? Do I have a severe case, or is it mild? Am I in remission? Is Tourette's remission even a thing? Am I on meds, and if so, what are they? How loud should my outbursts be? What is the proper cadence? Is it motherfucker, cocksucker, whore, and bastard, always in the same order, or should I mix it up? Do I occasionally throw in the C-word for effect? Do I have to bark every now and again? What about the N-word? That's off-limits, right? If I do use the N-word, I would have to fight the urge to lower my voice when I say it.

I was in deep.

Then I remembered that cursing is only one of the symptoms of Tourette's, and in fact, it's one of the rarer and more complex symptoms. In other words, I would have to display an array of some of the milder tics to go along with the cursing if I hoped to be authentic.

Maybe it was best to just come clean and humble myself. With all the sincerity I could muster, I could explain that it was a terrible attempt at a joke, how insensitive it was, and how sorry I am. If I really wanted to lay it on thick, I could say that this was a defining moment in my life and that I had learned a valuable lesson. I could even thank him for making me a better person.

Nah. I decided to continue the act, but I would find an excuse to leave after a couple of holes. On the first green, I teed up the ball, shrugged my shoulders a couple of times, blinked my eyes over and over, jerked my head, and practiced my swing more times than necessary.

I thought, *This is way too much. I am really an asshole. I have reached a new low in a lifetime of low moments. Now it's too late to apologize. I have to get out of here immediately.*

And then I hit the best drive of my life.

As I continued my sham, my second shot put me on the green. Then I drained an eighteen-foot putt. I birdied the first hole. I was in shock at my PGA-level performance.

Well, I can't leave now! As my symptoms worsened, my acting skills deserved an Oscar. I was having the best round of my life. Of course I finished all eighteen holes.

On the drive home, I started involuntarily screaming, "MOTH-ERFUCKING COCKSUCKER!" I realized that I played so well because I had been focusing on my faux Tourette's instead of my grip, stance, or swing. I knew then that if I wanted to play better golf, all I had to do is feign Tourette's every weekend.

Can I? Should I?

"MMMMMMMMOTHERFUCKER!"

Staging our House

The American Psychological Association ranks moving as one of the top five traumatic events in life. The death of a loved one is considered to be the most traumatic event, divorce is next, and in third place is moving. I have to believe that the stresses of moving can lead a person to divorce.

Thalia has always dreamed of living in a home on the water. After three years of Zillow alerts clogging up her inbox, her quest finally ended when she found the perfect house. In her wake, she left a trail of real estate agents, open houses, offers, attorneys, excitement, financial analysis, heartache, disappointment, and the last remnants of my sanity.

Thalia is an HGTV addict, and one of the biggest lessons she has learned is how important it is to properly stage a house before putting it up for sale. Even though I think we have lovely taste in furnishings, we hired a professional stager to guide us. She walked through the front door with an air of superiority and long, bony, arthritic fingers, and immediately shook her head. She started pointing out objects that had to be removed, which was pretty much everything we owned. After I made a flippant comment, she even pointed to me and added me to her "must-remove" list.

We were faced with the overwhelming task of stripping our house down to the bare minimum. We had already submitted an offer on another house, so time was of the essence. Since Thalia had beautifully decorated our home and added a lot of finishes, this was a major undertaking. She may have gotten her dream house, but it was the dawning of the age of Herman. The moon was in the seventh house, and Jupiter was aligned with Mars. Just as we were ready to start the purging process, I wound up in the hospital for emergency gallbladder surgery. *What a shame that I can't help*, I thought. I couldn't believe my good fortune—I didn't have to feign an injury or tap into my reservoir of excuses to get out of helping. Losing a major organ was a small price to pay. When the surgeon said that I was prohibited from lifting anything for six to eight weeks, I had to fight the urge to kiss the lips that uttered those words.

Thalia had to do everything on her own. Every day after work, at night, and on weekends, she was purging, sorting, organizing, wrapping, packing, and moving things. There was so much to do. I couldn't bear to see how hard she was working, so I would shut the bedroom door and turn up the volume on the TV set.

I had received a free pass, and not only did I take advantage of it at home, but I also used it to my benefit at work. Being an elder statesman in the office, I planned to exaggerate the depth and breadth of my wounds for as long as possible. Unfortunately, I got greedy and my fortunes shifted; ten days after my surgery, the managing partner in the firm also had his gallbladder removed. He was back to work in less than a week. I tried to explain that he was of Sicilian origin and came from sturdy stock, whereas my ancestors came from various ghettos and shtetls across Europe. His last name is affiliated with construction companies and waste management firms, while my people are medical patients with hospitals and clinics named after them. Of course our powers of recuperation would greatly differ. Sadly, my arguments were in vain and I had to return to the office.

Meanwhile, Thalia did an unbelievable job of decluttering the house. With over fifty cartons in her parents' basement and a ten-by-ten storage unit packed to capacity, our house looked better than it ever had. In fact, I was ready to suggest to Thalia that I wanted to love it instead of list it. (Fucking HGTV has breached my subconscious.)

Early in our marriage, I abdicated all decoration decisions to Thalia, giving her full reign and autonomy. Thalia being Thalia, she put the same energy and determination into staging our house that she had spent decorating it. She surpassed the expectations of the stager and began Thalia-izing the staging process, adding countless finishing touches. As a passenger in the process, I was just along for the ride. I rarely commented, merely nodding or shaking my head, and while I thought some of the things she did were unnecessary, I realized that this is who she is.

A few days before we were set to start showing the house, I took a shower and reached for my bathrobe. Instead of my aged velour bathrobe with the Parents Without Partners mismatched belt, I found a white, Four-Seasons-like robe on the hook. My wet skin was kissed by the plush terrycloth lining. I luxuriated in the thick, silky, soft fabric. I could wear this robe to the spa, while lounging around the pool, or while sitting on the veranda having a glass of wine with friends. As I pranced downstairs in my new robe to thank Thalia, I thought, *She is so thoughtful! I am a lucky man. In the middle of all this insanity, she found the time to buy me a present. I love it, and I love her.*

In the blink of an eye, Thalia was yelling at me. Apparently, that bathrobe was never intended for human consumption. Unbeknownst to me, I had put on the Staging Bathrobe. Thalia must have been afraid that no one would make an offer on our house because of our proletariat bathrobes. The robe thing was only the beginning. Towels that I wasn't allowed to use adorned the house. A new comforter that I wasn't allowed to sleep under graced our bed. I began to feel like I was living in a museum exhibit, forced to stand behind the cordoned-off sections so I wouldn't touch anything. Forget about finding any fucking thing that I needed in the house, as it was all hidden G-d knows where. Truth be told, I loved our house. I felt that whoever bought it was getting a bargain regardless of the sale price, and I was resentful of all the money we had poured into fixing it up. Despite my general crabbiness, I understood the need and tried not to complain too much.

After we repainted the house, refinished the hardwood floors, and performed assorted repairs and touch-ups, I thought we were finally done. We had done it all, there couldn't possibly be anything else to increase the appeal of the house. We did everything to justify our asking price: we removed clutter, arranged the furniture in a way that maximized the usable space, and ensured that the house had a flow. I was sure that prospective buyers could easily picture themselves living happily in our house. We'd done everything we possibly could. Or had we?

Not so, according to the stager. The toilet on the first floor was black, which appropriately fit the bathroom's motif. The stager commented that a black toilet would turn people off. I didn't understand. People couldn't picture themselves sitting on a black toilet? When I need a toilet, I don't care what color it is as long as there is reading material nearby. In fact, a black toilet is probably better because it hides stains.

Our house looked like the fucking Taj Mahal. We had upgraded and repaired, bought a new pump for the pond and a new filter for the pool, and power washed the pergola and backyard fence. Now we were expected to replace a perfectly good toilet? Apparently so, according to the stager. Not only did we have to buy a new toilet, but we also had to pay a plumber to install it. I felt like we were flushing away good money.

Luckily, our house sold in a single day for our asking price. Buyers did comment that they noticed that the toilet had been black in the listing photos, and they preferred the new, white one.

The shit had gotten real. We had sold our house and bought a new one, which meant we had to start packing over 3800 square feet and thirty-two years' worth of possessions in just two months. I quickly realized that decluttering our house for staging was just a dress rehearsal for the move. The task was daunting. Thalia and I prepared for packing and moving in our own ways. Thalia made lists, bought packing supplies, and called moving companies.

I, on the other hand, remembered how well the emergency gallbladder surgery had worked and decided to see if there were any other extraneous organs I could have removed. I called my son, the surgeon (not just a doctor, but a SURGEON!), to get a list of symptoms to feign. He mentioned something about a Hippocratic oath and suggested that I man up.

His advice fell on deaf ears. I knew I'd have to dig deep, tap into my inner Costanza, and come up with a Plan B.

The Best Job Interview

In 1977, I graduated magna cum laude from SUNY Albany with a double major in Marketing and Management. It was time to find a job and start my career.

I'd always wanted to go into advertising. In fact, my dream was to work for the firm of McMann & Tate. While I had a small thing for Laura Petrie as a kid, I was fully obsessed with Samantha Stephens in *Bewitched*, and I wanted to be Darrin/Darwin #3.

Through a college connection, I landed an interview with an ad agency and was offered a job as the assistant to an account executive. The only caveat was that I needed to be able to type fifty words per minute, which was a good thirty words faster than my best speed. They gave me a week to prepare before I was expected to come back to take a typing test. I checked two typing books for beginners out of the library, and for six days straight, all I did was practice on my family's old Royal typewriter. By Sunday evening, I was clocking in at more than sixty-five words per minute. I had calloused fingers, but I was ready.

The test was administered on a new IBM Selectric typewriter. On my thirty-year-old manual typewriter, I had to really push down on the keys with some force. Electric typewriters, on the other hand, were a tad more sensitive. I sneezed and three keystrokes appeared on the page. As I touched the first key, the letter T repeated across the page. Despondently, I looked at my hands, shook my head, and started again. I tried to tap each key as gingerly as possible, but to no avail. I realized at that point that I wwwaasss fffuuuckkkeddddddddddddddd.

Alas, I was not destined to name my future daughter Tabitha, as they informed me that they were going to fill the position with someone who possessed typing skills above the level of a rhesus monkey.

Dejectedly, I met with an employment agency whose mission was to find me a job, any job, as long as they could make a commission from it. They told me that my career should begin in a management training position. "Management training," while sounding impressive and correctly not included on the list of synonyms in *Roget's Thesaurus*, is in reality a "sales" position.

So there I was with a double major and a killer GPA, and the best they could do was to arrange an interview with Maidenform. My endless hours of studying and hard work were all for naught; I was interviewing to be an entry-level bra salesman.

I don't have anything against bras. As a matter of fact, I can fondly recall countless hours of direct, hands-on experience spent exploring every centimeter of them, trying in vain to unlock their mysteries. I just never thought I would be doing it professionally. After much soul searching, I told the agency that I didn't want to be a bra salesman. They assured me that it wasn't a sales position, but rather, I would be a "management trainee." That would make me a "management training bra salesman." Does that mean I would have a small territory to cover?

Reluctantly, I went on the interview.

As I waited in the lobby, scanning the Help Wanted section of *The New York Times*, I noticed a woman walk by. She was wearing only a bra and panties. A moment later, another woman walked by, similarly clad. The next thing I knew, a parade of models in various stages of undress sauntered through the lobby. I strategically placed *The Times* over my lap and made no pretense of not gawking. As I watched the gorgeous group of girls, I thought, *There is a G-d!* I was verklempt as every lingerie catalog I had under my bed growing up came to life and casually strolled by.

While I had always been a fan of the bra, I viewed it as a gateway garment. I knew that once I started experimenting with bras, I wouldn't be able to stop there. It would only lead to harder things. I'd never realized the multitude of different options that were available: strapless, push-up, padded, lace, full figure, underwire, bralette, halter, and even stick-on. They were all being proudly displayed for my viewing pleasure.

I'm ashamed to admit that I didn't play it cool. In fact, I was reduced to a childlike state. I was acting like the Count in *Sesame Street*: "One! One breast! Two! Three! Four! Four beautiful breasts! Ah-Ah-Ah! How many breasts can I count?" *It's ironic*, I thought, *that in college, I only wanted As. I was disappointed if I got a B. Now, all I want is to be surrounded by Cs and Ds!*

Eventually, the interviewer from HR came to get me. Holding my briefcase in front of me, I could only hope that he didn't notice how badly I wanted the job. Since his cubicle walls only went halfway up, I could still see the bevy of beauties during the interview.

The balding, middle-aged man before me seemed to take his job very seriously. The first question he asked me was, "What do you know about our products?" Without a second's hesitation, I responded, "Well, in the past, I have had trouble with your clasps." I thought, *Herm, you have hit it out of the ballpark!* I started to take my victory lap around the bases to the adulation of a cheering crowd. I was ready to negotiate my salary, compensation package, and set a starting date.

He sneered and wrote down my answer on his form. From the thrill of victory to the crushing agony of defeat. *Screw McMann and also Tate*, I thought, *I have found my passion and life's calling*. To redeem myself, I turned the tables and started asking him questions:

"What is your best seller and why?"

"What is the most popular cup size?"

"Isn't the Wonderbra false advertising?"

At the end of the interview, which he cut short, he asked if I had any final questions. I asked, "How much time do I have to spend in bras before I can get into the panties?"

The humorless man said the interview was officially over. I asked if it would be all right if I hung out in the inner lobby for a while. Rather than responding, he picked up his phone and called for security to escort me out of the building.

I didn't get the job and the employment agency dropped me as a client, but it wasn't all bad; I had the makings of a great story. In appreciation, I sent the human resources guy a short note that read, "Thanks for the mammaries."

Rickles 1 – Herman 0

Growing up white and Jewish on Long Island, which is where I developed my street savvy, my friends and I were into insult humor. After all, what else were white, Jewish kids capable of doing? Our hero was none other than the king of insults, Mr. Warmth, Don Rickles.

Rickles was known for singling out people in the audience and brutally insulting them. Nothing was sacred and no one was safe. Put an African American, Asian, Mexican, or fat man in the front row, and it was open season. My friends and I worshipped him.

I was caustic and fast. I dished it out all the time and got very little back in return. So it was fitting that for my fifteenth birthday, my parents got me front-row seats to see Rickles perform live at the Westbury Music Fair. I knew my destiny: Rickles was going to bring me up on stage. To prepare, I started writing material to insult him. I was going to go toe-to-toe with my hero. For hours upon hours, I practiced in front of the mirror. My friends would come over to help me rehearse, and by the night of the show, I was a fine-tuned machine. I was ready. Rickles was going down.

Halfway through the show, Rickles grabbed me by the arm and pulled me up on stage. As I stepped under the bright lights and onto the stage, I took a deep breath and thought, *This is it. This is your moment to shine. Show him what you've got!*

He shook my hand and asked, "What's your name, kid?"

Oh my G-d, I hadn't prepared for that question. In less than five seconds, he'd found the chink in my armor. Game, set, match. Dead Herman walking.

I didn't say anything. The way Rickles looked at me made me want to die. Finally, he said, "Are these questions too hard, dummy? Let's try again. Whattt isss yourrr name?"

I was so numb that I lost the power of speech. Rickles looked at the logo on my shirt, and said, "Lacoste? What are you, French?"

I couldn't delay any longer, so I feebly said, "My name is Herman."

He couldn't contain himself. As mucus flowed from his nose, he showered me in his DNA from laughing so hard. Between guffaws, he said, "Let me guess: Jewish, huh?"

For what seemed like an eternity but was actually more like ten straight minutes, Rickles spewed Herman jokes. He could barely breathe, the insults were coming so fast: the Garment District, gin rummy, the Fontainebleau in Miami Beach, bubbies, matzo balls, and every other Jewish stereotype possible.

And what a pity, I couldn't say a fucking word. The only sound I made was the sound of my testicles popping back inside my body.

Twenty years before they were brought to market, I developed the prototype for Depends, the adult diaper, while I stood impotently on stage. Finally, when he thought I'd had enough, I slithered back to my seat.

Thank G-d it was over . . . or was it? Whatever shred of dignity I had left was totally decimated during the remainder of his show. Every time he had the chance, Rickles referenced me in one form or another while attacking other people. I didn't know it at the time, but this evening would prove to be the catalyst for years of psychotherapy.

A few years ago, my friends and I went to a comedy club. I sat in the front row next to my friend Dennis, who decided to heckle the comedian. They were really going at it. Then, the comedian dragged me into the mess. He said, "You're this idiot's friend? What's your name?" I was plunged right back into my worst nightmare. I was fifteen again, up on stage with Rickles.

Droplets of urine started running down my leg. I froze as I felt the eyes of the comedian, my friends, and the audience all staring at me. Time stood still. How should I respond? Suddenly, it came to me. I thought, *Thank you, Don*, and I proudly shouted, "My name is Lacoste! It's French!"

How I Quit Smoking

When Thalia is finishing one project, she already has her next one mapped out, and usually the one after that too. I have benefited from her drive and vision over the years, so I wholeheartedly support her in all of her undertakings . . . except when it involves any participation on my part.

One spring day, Thalia declared that the landscaping in our yard needed a makeover. It had not even been a blip on my radar. Not only had I never thought about it, but when I examined the yard, I was more than satisfied with the existing landscaping. What wasn't to like? We had trees, some shrubs, flowers, stones, and plenty of green things. My definition of landscape work was hiring a member of one minority group, who brings in a truckload of members of another minority group to do the work. The extent of my involvement is opening my checkbook, reducing my risk of injury to a nasty paper cut.

To my horror, Thalia's definition included me doing physical labor. I carefully explained that my people don't do manual labor, and by *my people*, I mean professionals. (I didn't feel the situation warranted playing the Jewish card.) I thought I had successfully argued my point, but oh, how wrong I was.

When Memorial Day weekend came, a landscaping company dropped off two tons of rocks and pebbles, two tons of peat moss, a pile of mulch up to my waist, and two pallets of landscaping stones. Thalia's father came to help by doing the design work. He left everything else to me. I was no longer Herman Lentz with the great head of hair and rapier-like wit; I became Emanuel Labor, shoveling and schlepping. My neighbors looked on in astonishment, unable to believe what they were seeing. I was worried—if word got back to Temple Beth El, I would be shunned by the entire congregation.

It took me all three frigging days to complete the job. When I was finally done, I felt no sense of accomplishment, just anger and hostility. My body's once-virgin muscles were virgins no more. My skin, which was once soft and supple to the touch, was now calloused and rough. I needed a whole-body Band-Aid.

The following weekend, I was coerced into painting the back fence. My idea of painting a fence is similar to my thoughts on doing landscaping: grab my wallet and stay inside. But of course, Thalia had other thoughts.

In the middle of painting, I struggled to catch my breath, so I took a break to smoke a cigarette. My people aren't that bright either, and by *my people*, I mean nicotine addicts. At the time, I smoked two packs of Newport 100s a day. I loved smoking, and even though I knew how bad it was for me, I had no intention of quitting.

Shockingly, the cigarettes didn't help. I was having serious trouble breathing, so Thalia called our neighbor, who was a nurse. She took my vitals and immediately called 911. The next thing I knew, I was strapped to a gurney and there was an ambulance and two police cars in front of my house.

It was a beautiful, sunny day. Neighbors, little kids on bicycles, and people walking their dogs were all standing across the cul-de-sac, watching the spectacle. It was like they were filming an Allstate Insurance commercial. To add insult to injury, no one was commenting on the landscaping. Were all my efforts for naught? Had I worked myself into an early grave for nothing?

In the ambulance, every beep and buzz frayed my already frazzled nerves even further. I was terrified, sure that I was having a heart attack. I was rushed straight to the cardiac ER, where the medical team ran a battery of tests. After a long wait, the doctor told me it wasn't a heart attack.

Thank G-d.

And then it hit me: I have cancer. So, lying there in the ER, I made a deal with G-d. If I didn't have cancer, I would never touch another cigarette as long as I lived. They ran more tests, and it wasn't cancer.

Meanwhile, I still couldn't breathe. I was admitted, poked, prodded, X-rayed, and scanned. As I was lying in bed, a doctor came in with my chart in hand, hoping to speak with Thalia.

He said, "Mrs. Lentz, do you have any pets?"

She was confused, but eager to get to the bottom of things. "No, no pets."

"Ma'am, has your husband had any contact with animals recently?"

"Not to my knowledge. What's all this about?" she asked.

Rather curtly, the doctor asked Thalia to leave the room.

When she closed the door behind her, I said, "What's up, Doc?"

The doctor looked at me with repulsion and total disgust. With a sneer, he said, "I'm not judging you, but I need you to be honest with me, sir. Mr. Lentz, have you had . . . relations with an animal?"

What the hell? I thought. My people definitely don't do that, and by *my people*, I mean men who don't have gerbil races in their rectum. I was relieved that I hadn't suffered a heart attack, nor was my body riddled with cancer. I felt stronger, and my snarky powers were returning in full force, so I said, "Well, I have called my wife Lamb Chop and Lambykins in the past. Does that count?"

"Mr. Lentz, you have animal spores in your system. How did they get there?"

I was stunned. I didn't even know what an animal spore was! I began to wonder if I had ended up with a guy who only became a medical doctor after he flunked out of veterinary school.

"Mr. Lentz, I am serious. Did you have sex with an animal?"

"Well, Doc, there was this one girl in college who was pretty wild and kinky. She was definitely animal-like."

He just shook his head and walked out of the room.

Thalia returned and asked me about what the doctor said.

"Thalia, you're not going to believe this. He asked me if I had sex with an animal!"

She thought I was kidding. "Did you tell him about that girl in college?"

"Thalia, this is serious. There are animal spores in my system, and I have no idea how they got there." *Maybe she had sex with an animal*, I thought. *I could have caught it from her.* I quickly decided against accusing her. After all, I was already in the hospital and in a weakened state. I didn't need her to do anything to worsen my condition.

I had no idea what was going through her head. Was she eyeing me suspiciously? If I were to watch the Westminster Dog Show, would she think I'm into puppy porn? And forget about taking Jimmy and Jonathon to the local petting zoo. Even the name sounded repulsive. Would I have to register with the local authorities before I visit the Bronx Zoo?

Later that day, a different doctor came in to see me. He broke the news that I had double pneumonia. Thank G-d!

I said, "The last doctor told me I have animal spores in my system, and he wanted to know if I had sex with an animal. I didn't, Doc, just for the record."

He checked my chart and confirmed that spores were indeed present. "Surely there's a reasonable explanation that doesn't involve bestiality, Mr. Lentz. Have you been camping recently?"

Me? Camping? Can you imagine such a thing?

"Can you think of anything you've done that is out of the ordinary?"

"Seriously, Doc, my idea of roughing it is staying at a three-star hotel. The closest I've gotten is some yard work last weekend." I described the tons of rocks, pebbles, and peat moss, the Mount Everest of mulch, and the pallets of landscaping stones that stretched as far as the eye could see.

Lucky for me, this doctor wasn't Jewish and instantly realized the cause of my problem. He informed me that peat moss has animal spores in it. (There is no way a Jewish doctor would have made that connection, or would ever go camping, for that matter.)

Well, I ended up spending more than a week in the hospital, and for the first few days, I was on oxygen. In time, I made a full recovery. This happened over thirty years ago, and I have upheld my promise to the Big Guy: I never touched another cigarette. I know that if I had even one, I would start smoking again.

In the three decades since that fateful hospital trip, we have owned five dogs, the majority of which were female. While I do love them and enjoy snuggling with them on my bed, my feelings are always strictly platonic.

Lasagna

I am the worst person to invite over for dinner. I have issues, to say the least. While I consider myself to be charming and wonderful company, and I actively partake in the banter and clever repartee at the dinner table, I am a fussy eater and nearly impossible to cook for.

Issue #1: If I can't hug it, I won't eat it. You can't hug a fish, so anything that swims or crawls or lives in water is out. Veal parmigiana, on the other hand, is my absolute favorite and would be my last meal before going to the electric chair. Young calves are highly huggable, and on their atrophied little legs, those delicious darlings can't run away from you, so you can mosey on over and throw your arms around 'em.

My limited diet and finickiness have profoundly impacted my life, and worse yet, I've made Thalia complicit in a cover-up. She's perjured herself for me. When Thalia and I toured China, I packed a suitcase full of Pop-Tarts since I realized that meals in a foreign country would be a problem. Not wanting me to explain my "hug it or leave it" policy at every meal, Thalia decided to tell everyone on our tour that I was severely allergic to seafood. I'm not sure if it was totally for my benefit or if she just didn't want to be embarrassed by the man she has chosen to spend her life with and his totally absurd philosophy.

Panic set in one night when a fellow traveler noticed that I had mistakenly taken a bite of a shrimp egg roll. After frantically checking my pockets, I screamed to Thalia for my nonexistent EpiPen. I didn't know what to do when she said she didn't have it with her. Fucking Thalia. I ran to the bathroom and thought how lucky I was that there were no prepubescent children on the trip who were armed with an EpiPen. After splashing water on my face, tousling my hair, and untucking my shirt, I emerged from the bathroom looking appropriately disheveled. I thanked the group for their concern and reassured them it had been a close call but I would be okay. I knew that the price for Thalia's silence would probably mean doubling her jewelry budget for the trip.

Issue #2: Where's the beef? Even with my "hug it or leave it" rule, there are caveats. I will only eat food from the top level of the huggable food chain. Bambi is huggable, so venison is a popular dish in my house. But given the choice between an aged filet mignon that is so tender I can cut it with a dull butter knife and roadkill deer steak that is gamey at best, my selection is a no-brainer. I will only eat prime cuts of meat. Even hamburger meat has to be at least 90 percent lean. I cringe when I am served a steak that is laden with fat and gristle. With laser-like precision, I dissect it and remove all traces of the offending matter before I take my first bite.

Issue #3: Hiding the evidence. After I complete my meat surgery, I am faced with the dilemma of what to do with the remains. When I scan the table, all I can see are the empty plates of my fellow diners. Meanwhile, mine looks like the floor of a slaughterhouse. Not wanting to offend the host or bring additional attention to myself, I will place my napkin over my plate with the magical skills of Houdini, hoping to create the illusion that the remains have disappeared.

Issue #4: Most Fowl is Foul. Chicken and turkey are the only fowl I will eat, but I scrutinize my plate carefully. I don't want to sound like a misogynist, but I am a breast man, and I don't want to sound racially insensitive, but I will only eat white meat. I have watched in horror as cannibalistic people lick their fingers after devouring the cartilage, bones, and gristle of chicken wings. Prior to my discovery of boneless chicken wings, I was limited to dipping the few pieces of decorative celery into the blue cheese dressing at Super Bowl parties.

And for the record, a turkey meatball is not a meatball. It is an offensive and gross injustice to pasta. After all, no one says, "I want a meat meatball."

Issue #5: Nothing Exotic. Every time I hear someone say that they had frog legs, rabbit, or rattlesnake and that it tasted just like chicken, I want to hit them. You know what else tastes just like chicken? Chicken!

I'm not alone in my aversion to exotic meats. Like most sensible people, I refuse to be experimental and try alligator, kangaroo, wild boar, or ostrich. Personally, I add non-kosher hot dogs to the list. Goy-Dogs, as I refer to them, are not made of actual meat, but of meat byproducts, including but not limited to pig anuses. I watch in disgust whenever someone eats a hot dog from a street vendor in

New York. I get sick every year when they televise the Nathan's Hot Dog Eating Contest on the Fourth of July.

Even though I am not kosher, I believe that when the learned rabbis and Jewish scholars sat around a fig tree in the Holy Land three thousand years ago to debate and codify the Jewish dietary laws, bacon cheeseburgers would have replaced broiled chicken as the Friday night Sabbath meal if crispy bacon had been available at the time.

Issue #6: The Sanctity of Caffeine. I insist on topping off every meal with a cup of coffee. I am a caffeine junkie, and I love a good hot cup of coffee after a meal. I recoil in revulsion when anyone asks if I want regular or decaf. What's the point of drinking decaf? It's just coffee with a vasectomy!

Not only does coffee appeal to my sense of taste, but I also take pleasure in the olfactory experience. With each sip, I breathe in the aroma of the brew. Flavored coffee's sickly-sweet smell is an insult to the bean. Each cup of flavored coffee should be served with a tiny umbrella in it. French vanilla, hazelnut, caramel, pumpkin spice—is there no end to the degradation of the nectar of the g-ds?

I realize my issues have not only impacted my life, but my family's as well. I can offer no rational excuse for my behavior, but being Jewish, that's not a problem. I will lay full blame on my mother.

Everyone tells me that Thalia is a great cook, but unfortunately, her talents are wasted on me and my limited palate. When we were first married, Thalia wanted to share her heritage and prepared a lot of Greek dishes for me, sans fish, of course. I have a Semitic gastrointestinal tract that was not accustomed to Greek cuisine, which consists of a lot of fried food. As it is, Jews are seen by gastroenterologists more than any other group. Imagine adding a fried-food diet to the mix!

Instead of lying on sheets at night, we should lie on brown paper bags to soak up the oil as it drains from our bodies. Rightfully so, Thalia has given up and we eat a lot of preprepared food. My response to hearing a microwave beep has become a textbook example of classical conditioning. Any time I hear the microwave chime, day or night, I start to salivate, look for silverware, and walk to the table for dinner.

I would like to think that my idiosyncrasies have shaped my sons into the men they are today. Witnessing my limited palate motivated James to become an Executive Chef, dedicating his life to creating dishes that I find appetizing. Watching the skill and precision I use to dissect a steak inspired Jon to become a talented surgeon.

My diet also affects our social life; being invited to a friend's house for dinner is a particular challenge. Thalia has to cover for me and ask what the host is making ahead of time. After years of restrictions and countless dining disasters, I finally had the perfect meal. Our friends, Jim and Andre, invited us over for dinner, and as expected, Thalia reviewed the menu with Jim beforehand. We were going to start off with a Caesar salad. Thalia reminded Jim that the anchovies had to be on the side, and when placing the disgusting little fish on the table, Jim must ensure that they are out of my line of sight. For the main course, Jim was preparing a lasagna. Thalia discussed the ingredients with Jim. Pasta: check. Ricotta cheese: check. Tomato sauce: check. Sausage and lean ground beef: check. There was nothing on my no-eat list. Dinner was a go!

The cheese was oozing out the sides, the noodles were slightly crisp, and the ragù was to die for. It was one of the best meals I had ever eaten. Every bite was pure heaven. Normally, because of my dietary limitations, I avoid taking second helpings. On this glorious day, my second serving was larger than my first.

The exquisite gastronomic masterpiece had delighted my senses and made my stomach so very happy. In the span of a single evening, I had fallen in love with Jim. I had to thank him. "Jim, this is one of the best meals I've ever had. Thank you, you are spoiling me. Even Thalia is not this good to me."

Jim, who takes great pleasure in teasing me, gave me a dramatic wink. "Well, if you should ever decide to switch teams, I would cook for you all the time."

I laughed and responded, "You never know, Jim. If this meal is an example of your culinary skills, you might have yourself a deal. Should anything ever happen to Thalia and Andre, perhaps they both get trampled in a stampede at Home Goods, who knows what could happen?"

Thalia overheard part of the conversation and asked what we were talking about. Before I had a chance to reply, Jim chimed in. "Herman just offered me a blow job in exchange for my lasagna."

As the three of them made jokes at my expense, all I could do was gag. I mean, it was good, but really, oral sex for lasagna? No way. And then I thought, *Thank G-d he didn't make veal parm!*

Bonsai

Bonsai – The Japanese art of pruning and training dwarfed trees in a pot to produce a desired shape or effect.

Banzai – The battle cry shouted by Japanese kamikaze pilots as they attacked enemy forces during a suicide mission.

Hazarai – A Yiddish expression often used to describe junk, nonsense, or bullshit.

Thalia's birthday was approaching, and I was faced with the dilemma of what to buy her. I knew I was an enabler and fed her habit, and despite the cost, she couldn't get enough of the finer things. It started out innocently enough with the gift of a Louis Vuitton wallet. It was a tad expensive, but Thalia is worth it.

Then she craved the LV handbag to put the LV wallet in. The handbag became the gateway purchase in her years-long Louie addiction. Where else would she put her credit cards but in an LV card holder? It was only slightly larger than her LV change purse, but it was a must-have. She didn't want the Louie briefcase; the Louie knapsack would suffice.

Over the years, Thalia became a magician, able to pull a Louie out of a Louie out of another Louie. The Vuitton cartel kept pushing increasingly expensive products to feed her out-of-control addiction. When she started to look at a Louie trunk to store all of her Louies, I considered staging an intervention. So, with her birthday fast approaching, I set out on a kamikaze mission to find a non-Vuitton birthday present for her. Banzai!

Thalia's talents and energy know no bounds. Over the forty years of our marriage, she has taken on and mastered a long list of passion projects. One of the most recent is the succulent breeding farm we have in our house. What started years ago as a wedding favor for our son has developed into an orphanage for succulent plants, consisting of a custom-built table, twenty-four-hour grow lamps, and boundless maternal love and devotion.

In passing, she'd mentioned that she wanted really good pruning tools for her succulents. Bingo! I went shopping online for really good pruning tools for succulents, but I stumped Google and came up empty on Amazon. Luckily, I consider myself to be a semi-creative person. Actually, I consider myself brilliant, but since I'm also exceptionally humble, I'll stick with semi-creative. Since they don't sell really good pruning tools for succulents, I went searching for a substitute. And then it hit me: bonsai tools. Perhaps my mission was not suicidal after all.

I was suddenly flooded with choices: bonsai tools for beginners, ten-piece sets, thirty-five-piece sets, carbon steel sets, one-hundred-piece sets, sets with carrying cases, designer sets. The list went on and on. Knowing Thalia, I based my selection solely on price. Experience has taught me that she would not be happy with anything on the lower end of the price spectrum. On the other hand, I knew I would not be happy with anything on the higher end of the spectrum. That left the middle, but not the middle-middle. I had to start at the upper-middle, which is ultimately where I ended up. I was the exception, the one kamikaze pilot who lived to tell the tale of his mission. I had a non-Vuitton birthday present for Thalia that was in a price range we both found acceptable.

Despite the fact that I never received a "World's Greatest Dad" mug, I knew that every year, James and Jon would take out loans to chip in for Thalia's next Louie. Since I really am the world's greatest dad, mug or no mug, I decided to throw them a bone. I suggested that they each buy her a bonsai tree. After all, why not? She now has an upper-middle range bonsai tool kit, why not maximize its potential?

Without a moment's hesitation, they both agreed. When would I learn to leave well enough alone? It's a character flaw of mine that I need to work on. I volunteered to place the order for them, which they also agreed to instantly. So back I went to Amazon to search for bonsai trees.

While she still has the ability to surprise me, I am well versed in the ways of Thalia after four decades of marriage. One of her superstitions is that you simply can't have an even number of things (don't ask, don't know, can't even guess). I realized that I couldn't just order one bonsai tree for each of the boys; I needed to order three because she would inevitably order a third to have an odd number, and it would be more expensive than the one I would have picked out.

Now I had to find three suitable bonsai trees. I wondered, *How did I get myself into this mess?* I was beginning to regret the fact that I had ordered the upper-middle bonsai tool kit; with the cost of the third tree, I might have gotten away with the middle-middle kit. Reluctantly, I ordered three bonsai trees from a national floral chain. With late deliveries and damaged plants, they totally screwed up the order. Every time I called their customer service department, their excuses amounted to a lot of hazarai.

I became possessed on my mission. I *would* have satisfaction. I wouldn't deal with the first line of defense of customer service reps, I demanded to speak to the supervisor's supervisor. With dogged determination, I complained about every screw-up and broken promise. Eventually, they relented. For a total investment of $150, I ended up with not three but five bonsai and $100 in gift certificates. A win for the kid. Despite how good I felt, I knew there would be a price to pay. I had surely been flagged in many a database in India as an unreasonable schmuck, so I would fear for my safety in the great subcontinent. So much for seeing the Taj Mahal.

As it turned out, Thalia did not like the feel of the carbonized steel, upper-middle range bonsai tool kit I had thoughtfully selected, so I returned it. She has not replaced it.

What about a happy ending? Had I learned nothing? I found myself laden with explosives, dive bombing straight toward the deck of an aircraft carrier. I had introduced five bonsai into the house; of course, they cannot just sit on a random table, shelf, or windowsill. How pedestrian of me to think that. Naturally, they needed to be positioned in alignment with the house's Feng Shui, presented in a way that meets Thalia's discerning design criteria.

To that end, Thalia ordered a six-foot Oriental display table for $750, faster than she could say bonsai.

When it came unassembled, I chanted banzai.

The plants died a few months later because they were hazarai.

The leaves had fallen from the trees, and the holiday season was fast approaching. Once again, it was the dreaded gift-giving time. For some reason, I found myself thinking about the lyrics to "Brother Louie" by the Stories.

Louie Louie Louie Louie

Louie Louie Louie Lou I

Louie Louie Louie Louie

Louie Louie I'm gonna buy

Witchi-Tai-To

When I was fifteen years old, I thought I was going to die. Thanks to centuries of breeding, my threshold for pain was minimal; I was in agony and could barely walk. I looked like the Elephant Man as I limped home. It was the worst pain I had ever experienced.

I was returning home from my girlfriend's house. We had just finished our first make-out session on the couch in her basement. I had played spin the bottle and seven minutes in heaven at parties before, but this experience was totally different. Although we were horizontal, parts of me were vertical.

Pam (not her real name, as I don't know how long the statute of limitations lasts) was my first love. We met at temple youth group. She was beautiful, had long, auburn hair, an inviting smile, and she found me funny, which was one of her most attractive features. I don't want to sound misogynistic, but her features were very age appropriate—to my fifteen-year-old body, ravaged by raging hormones, they were practically like Mount Everest.

Pam and I spent a lot of afternoons hanging out in her basement, listening to music. I loved that basement. It had wood paneling, a linoleum floor, a Ping-Pong table, a console stereo, and a couch. Her dad's record collection included the likes of Perry Como and Andy Williams. I didn't particularly like that old-fashioned music, but realizing my good fortune of being in that basement in the first place, I would have listened to Gregorian monks chanting.

Every album cover featured men in blazers or turtlenecks and ladies in evening gowns and gloves. We chanced upon one album that had a picture of two unkempt younger guys with long hair and mustaches, and one was even wearing a Panama hat. We gave it a spin. The album was by Brewer & Shipley, an American folk-rock duo. They are best known for their song, "One Toke Over the Line." They quickly became my favorite group.

I'll never forget that first afternoon in her basement. We started kissing, and before long, it was clear that we both wanted more. Being completely inexperienced in this area, my multiple attempts to remove her bra were futile; the hooks totally thwarted me. I was nervous because it was the closest I had ever gotten. My previous efforts with girls had all been met with dazzling displays of martial arts defensive moves that would have made Bruce Lee proud.

With Pam, I was so close yet so far. Had there been a pair of scissors nearby, I would have just cut the damn bra off. Fearing that my fumbling would lead to a spinal injury, she assisted me, but by then, the mood was thoroughly ruined. And thus, my painful walk home. I had no idea what was happening to me. I couldn't recall any episode of *Marcus Welby, M.D.* in which a patient presented with the symptoms

I was experiencing. Maybe Nurse Consuelo took care of those poor bastards. Had WebMD existed at the time, I would have discovered that I was suffering from epididymal hypertension, which sounds so much better than the more commonly known term: blue balls.

I made it home and went straight to my room. My mother's Jewish Spidey senses were tingling. She asked me what was wrong, ready to admit me to the Mayo Clinic. A chat with my mother was not the conversation I wanted to have at the time. I took matters into my own hands, so to speak, and although I was late for dinner, I recovered with no lasting effects.

Pam and I kept seeing each other. Our kissing and groping progressed to outercourse, which sounds so much cooler than *dry humping*. We probably looked like two Amish people trying to dance at first, but we quickly found our rhythm. While we were culminating our act, Brewer & Shipley were belting out "Witchi-Tai-To" in the background. I would love to brag and say I lasted all the way through "In-A-Gadda-Da-Vida" by Iron Butterfly, which is over seventeen minutes long, but I would be lying. For my first time with Pam, the Happy Birthday song would have sufficed. "Witchi-Tai-To" was a respectable seven minutes long and came to a crescendo at the end.

They say love can move mountains. Teenage lust and vigor, on the other hand, can move a couch on wheels. After a while, we noticed that it had left scuff marks on the linoleum floor. I guess I had only one move at the time, as the scuff marks were not random but followed a pretty consistent path.

I went over to Pam's house every day after school. She always asked what I wanted to do, and my response was the same each day: "I dunno. What do you wanna do? How about listening to some Brewer

& Shipley?" I still can't believe I never tripped running down the basement stairs.

While I truly loved Brewer & Shipley, I got greedy after a few months and wanted to sample other musical styles. Unfortunately, Pam found out and broke up with me.

Years later, when I was a student at Boston University, I took Psychology 101 and learned about Pavlov's classical conditioning. This form of unconscious learning happens when a biologically potent stimulus (kissing and heavy petting) is paired with a neutral stimulus (the music of Brewer & Shipley) to form a learned response. To this day, when I hear the song "Witchi-Tai-To," I do more than smile.

The Wedding Speech

John and Louis, my dear friends, asked me to speak at their wedding. I said I would be honored to say a few words during the reception. To my surprise, they told me they wanted me to give a speech during the ceremony.

Ceremony?

Panic set in. I had no idea what to say. As a Long Island Jew, I'm not totally at ease in a church. The thought of giving a speech at this most special of all occasions was quite intimidating. I double checked with John to make sure he had thought his request through carefully. He said he was sure. I asked him if there was anything in particular he wanted me to cover, but he just wanted me to be myself. Oy!

For three days straight, I racked my brain but came up empty. Between the psalms, hymns, and benedictions, Shecky Lentz would be doing schtick in a house of worship for over two hundred of John and Louis's family and friends. What if I bomb? Everywhere you look inside a church, you can see what happened to another famous Jew. It doesn't look all that pleasant.

I wondered how I could put my own spin on the speech. It had to be poignant and sincere, yet light and funny at the same time. I needed to capture their essence and devotion to each other without making it too schmaltzy. *Should I acknowledge that it's a gay wedding? If so, how can I strike the right tone?* I realized I couldn't make a joke about it; that would just be wrong and in really bad taste.

Perhaps I should just talk about the two of them and what makes their relationship so special. Louis clearly adores John, and without question, John also clearly adores John. John is complex: he's a gay man who loves women's breasts. Could I do anything with that? Then I realized that this was meant to be a wedding speech and not a Friars Club roast. As hard as I tried, I still had no clue where to start.

Finally, I gave up. Instead of trying to write a speech, I spent more time and effort coming up with an excuse to get out of it. I was in turmoil. As I reflected on the best way to handle the sticky situation, I had an epiphany. John and Louis had asked me to speak during their wedding ceremony, and since it was going to be held in a church—which is not really G-d's primary residence, but more like his summer home—I had to be respectful. I couldn't rely on clever wordplay or dazzle the audience with my trademark witticism. I went to bed knowing what I had to do. Even though it might be bland, my speech would come from the heart and show the kinder, gentler side of my nature. I was relieved.

But then, I woke up in the middle of the night, my head swirling with ideas. I stumbled to my computer with a sly, sleepy smile, typed, "Burning Bush," and went back to bed.

The Speech

I was honored when Louis and John asked me to speak at their wedding. Thank you both very much. I know they were hoping that I would be funny, but instead, I'm going to play it straight, which I realize may not be a popular choice here today.

I thought it would be appropriate to begin with a passage from the Gospels. I had considered pulling from Romans or Corinthians, but being Jewish, I am more comfortable with the original version of the Bible and not the sequel. So, for today's reading, I chose the Book of John. This is not from John the Baptist, but John the Prignano.

The passage is from John 1, "And on the Eighth Day." And John reacheth into his pocket and could not find his cell phone. He commandeth, "Louis, where art my cell phone?" And forth came Louis, with a heart that is pure and a love that knows no bounds. Louis reached down to the couch right next to where John was sitting and picked up John's cell phone, and with a smile upon his face, Louis kissed John on the forehead and handeth the missing phone to him.

And as John grew bored and wanted to view another show, the remote was not to be found. Again, he summoned forth Louis, and said unto him, "Louis where did thou put thy remote? How can I changeth the channel without my remote?" And Louis, who sees beauty where others do not, who, thank the heavens, only sees the good in people, asked John with compassion and understanding, "John, doest thou sitteth upon the remote again?"

And as John surveyed his holdings, all 905 square feet, he wanted to gaze upon all that was his. With righteous indignation, he bellowed, "Louis, where art my glasses? I shant see all of my wealth and worldly possessions without my glasses." And Louis looked at John, and his voice sounded as if a choir of angels in Heaven were singing. "Mooshkie, my little lambkin, it is as clear as the nose on your face, which is exactly where your glasses are, resting on thy nose upon thy face. Thou art such a silly little bear."

And John, sitting on his couch of leather, looked upon all the things that Louis does for him, and John sayeth, "Louis is good."

And thus concludes the passages from the Book of John. Now I'd like to tell you the story of John the Prignano. In biblical times, John was walking along a mountain path, and he chanced upon a burning bush. And John kept walking, as he was not interested in the bush.

When the Israelites heard of this, many asked, "John, what is wrong with you? You weren't moved by a bush, especially one that is burning?"

And John said, "No, a burning bush does nothing for me." And then John added, "But if Moses were to traipse down the mountain with his flowing beard and perfectly coiffed salt-and-pepper hair, yummmmm, me likey!"

And the children of Israel couldn't understand it. They thought John was odd. But there were many in the group who felt the same way, that a bush, burning or not, was unappealing. They became John's disciples.

In his high-heeled sandals and designer robe of many colors, John traveled throughout the lands, preaching his gospel of loving thy fellow man. John's message was simple. He would single out one person in the crowd, and he would say, "Young man, there's no need to feel down. I said, young man, pick yourself off the ground." And those who dwelled in the cities found truth in his words, and the people who lived in the towns understood. And for the Village People, it became their credo, passed on from generation to generation.

At the end of his sermon, John would pull out his rod, raise it aloft for all to see, and say to the crowd, "Behold my mighty rod." And upon seeing it, the masses would shudder and tremble. Word spread about John's rod, and his following grew. They were diverse. They included women who only worshipped the burning bush, men who didn't care for the burning bush, and those who sometimes liked it and sometimes did not.

John's disciples came from all walks of life, for his message resonated with all: the rich, the poor, the intellectuals, the common man, the infirmed, the slow, the dimwitted, and even the boobs. Of all his followers, John's favorite were the boobs. He didn't understand why, as it didn't make any sense, but John really loved the boobs. He spent a vast amount of time staring at them and smiling. If given the opportunity, he would hug the boobs and play with them, as John was an affectionate man.

As John wandered the desert, new tribes joined his flock. There were the "Lovers of Liza," "Jews for Judy," and "Barbara's Bitches." Even members of nearby guilds worshipped him, like the carpet and rug merchants, the cobblers of comfortable footwear, and of course, just about everyone from the performing arts.

But alas, something was missing in his life. John knew he was incomplete.

Then one fateful day, John was walking along the mountain path, when suddenly an angel appeared from the heavens. And this angel looked at John and said unto him, "Hola poochie, me llamo Louis. I am the healer of the sick, the trader of antiquities. Your search is over, I will be your partner and we shall both be complete."

And let us all say, "Amen."

The Thrill of Victory, The Agony of De-foot

As I was clearing my driveway after a snowstorm, I was thankful that my snow blower was working; I always said a prayer to the deities when I attempted to start it up for the first time in a season. Hoping that no one from Temple Beth El would see me since this act could be grounds for excommunication, I understood why Jews migrate to Florida for the winter. I was not bred for shoveling or plowing snow, or for any form of physical labor, for that matter.

Thalia shares my aversion to the cold. Although she was born and grew up in Montreal, she was conceived in Greece and has warm, Mediterranean blood flowing through her veins. At the first sign of a frost, she goes into hibernation mode. If it weren't for online shopping, she wouldn't survive the winter months.

Given our shared distaste for the cold, it came as quite a surprise when Jimmy and Jonathon became snowboarding junkies. Every winter, I took the boys on a variety of day and weekend trips, and even a few weeklong snowboarding vacations. Most of the time, Thalia stayed home, unwilling to intentionally subject herself to the cold if it wasn't absolutely necessary.

I usually sat in the lodge and did paperwork while the boys hit the slopes. After a few years, I decided that I should be out there making memories and frolicking with my boys instead of sitting on my ass and doing work. So, I decided to learn how to ski.

The first step in the process was looking the part. I made a trip to Ski Barn, which proved to be a tad more expensive than I expected. I purchased top shelf: long underwear, fleece tops, ski socks, ski gloves, goggles, neck gaiter, and an insulated, waterproof, vented, down jacket with matching ski pants. *I may be a beginner, but damn it, I am going to look good.* Picture it: a snowy slope touched by the first warm rays of sunshine, skiers and snowboarders negotiating the trails—a true winter wonderland. And there I was, right in the middle of it all, on my skis and dressed to the nines.

One year, we went on an overnight trip to Mount Snow with Thalia's cousin Bobby, his wife Paula, and their four kids. Everyone in that family was an experienced skier or snowboarder. Shockingly, Thalia joined us for the trip. Her intent was not to turn the Lentzes into the von Trapp family, singing and skiing down the mountain together to escape the Nazis. No, her intentions were more nefarious. Only a short drive from Mount Snow is the Crossings Premium Outlets, which features over one hundred designer and name brand outlet stores offering up to 65 percent savings. Thalia and Paula were eager to shop till they dropped.

We both set out on our missions for the day: I was determined to conquer a mountain, and Thalia resolved to peruse the offerings in every store. Since she knew that I'm inherently clumsy and my athletic prowess left something to be desired, Thalia told me to be careful and not hurt myself. I scoffed at the notion. Seeing that I obviously wasn't taking her seriously, she listed some of my previous exploits, including breaking my finger trying to catch a baseball with my throwing hand and not with my glove; needing a cortisone shot for the tennis elbow I developed after buying an Atari 2600 and getting addicted to virtual golf; and being relegated to only using a Tonka toy toolbelt after multiple mishaps around the house. I assured her that I would be fine, and we each went on our way.

I signed up for group lessons, rented my equipment, and eagerly made my way to the ski school area. As I envisioned myself gracefully swooshing down the mountain, I was certain I'd be a naturally gifted skier. I made my way through the chaos of the Powder Pandas class for ages three to four, the Grizzlies, age five to seven, and the snowboarder area, where everyone looked like they belonged to a grunge band from Seattle. Finally, I found the section for adult beginners. The ragtag group comprised a collection of every person picked last for a sports team.

Surveying this eclectic group and their diverse outfits, I had to believe that a bus must have picked them up from a homeless shelter for a day trip to the slopes. It may have been unfair of me, but my ensemble and I didn't fit in with this group of misfits, so I decided to enroll in two days of private lessons instead.

By the end of the first morning, my instructor was very happy with my progress. He told me to spend the afternoon practicing what I'd learned and suggested that we meet again the next morning to start attempting the trails. With his words of encouragement ringing in my frostbitten ears, I proceeded to the Killer Hare Trail (a.k.a. the Bunny Trail) to hone my newly developed skills.

My first few moments were a bit clumsy, like a newborn fawn, but before long, I was actually skiing. As I was snowplowing and taking wide, sweeping turns, I thought, *This is fun! Everything is coming together. I was born to ski!* Just then, a woman came down the trail, out of control. Before I could get out of the way, she crashed squarely into me. When I looked down, I saw that my boot was perpendicular to my leg.

As she rose to her feet, she nonchalantly asked if I was okay. I yelled, "Look at my fucking foot! Does that look okay?" I gathered myself, took a steadying breath, and said, "My ankle is probably broken. Please go get ski patrol so I can get some help."

She shrugged. "I'll try, but I have to get back to the bus before it leaves. See ya!"

Had there been cell phones at the time, I would have been on the phone with personal injury attorneys Morgan & Morgan so fast it would've made her head spin. I'd have sued the bitch for all she was worth, which, judging by her outfit, wasn't much. She skied off before I could get her license and registration.

Ski patrol came with a stretcher attached to a snowmobile and carted me off to the infirmary. They didn't need an x-ray or advanced medical degree to tell me that my ankle was broken; the only question was how badly it was broken. I wondered, *Is there a good way to break your ankle?* As they struggled to remove my boot, I was inventing new curse words. Loudly. Having an extremely low threshold for pain to begin with, actually enduring something painful was beyond my coping skills. They called for an ambulance to take me to the hospital.

Unfortunately, there was a small problem: Jimmy and Jona-thon were still on the mountain with Bobby and his kids. They had no idea that I'd been in an accident, so I needed to get word to them. The patrol said they would page Bobby. I said, "His last name is Four-niadis, but I don't know how to spell it." It turned into a gigantic problem. It was like the speed round of *Wheel of Fortune*, and I was screaming out random letters and vowels.

Finally they gave up and just made the announcement. "Would Bobby Fuckingitis please report to the infirmary?" To my absolute shock, Bobby showed up. With his four kids and my two in tow, he arrived at the infirmary just as the ambulance was pulling up. The paramedics asked if Bobby would be joining me at the hospital. After putting it to a vote, everyone decided to stay on the mountain. The results were unanimous. *With friends like these, who needs enemies?*

I made it to the hospital with no trouble, and the x-ray confirmed that my ankle was broken in two places. As I lay in the hospital bed with my foot in traction and morphine flowing through my veins, I envisioned Thalia's face staring at me with her "I told you so" look. *How am I going to explain this one?* I tried coming up with an excuse, but even in my opioid-induced state, I had nothing. I knew I'd be hearing about this for years to come.

Then I realized what had really happened. My Italian friends call it il malocchio, the Greeks call it the mati, and my fellow Jews say Kinna Hurra. They all mean the same thing: the evil eye. If Thalia hadn't told me to be careful and not get hurt, that homeless woman would have missed the bus that morning. She had cursed me! I convinced myself that everything was Thalia's fault. I knew I would forgive her eventually, but it might take some time.

Meanwhile, Thalia's day was more successful than mine. In fact, she was close to meeting her shopping quota for the year. When Bobby told her that I was in the hospital with a broken ankle, she didn't believe him. Knowing my sense of humor, Thalia thought that I was playing an elaborate prank on her. She later told me that as she was pulling into the hospital parking lot, she felt impressed by my dedication to my craft and how far I was willing to go for a joke and to prove her wrong. I had to admit that making her go all the way to the hospital just to prove her wrong would have been a brilliant joke.

When she walked in and saw me lying in a hospital bed with my foot in a cast attached to some contraption up in the air, she started to laugh. Since I could feel no pain, I joined in her laughter. This is not to say that Thalia lacks compassion; she is very empathetic and caring. Nor do I mean to imply that she found humor in my broken ankle or the fact that I was in pain. Based on my history, she felt that I was destined to break something, so her laughter was in relief that I wasn't in a full-body cast.

In the end, my ankle healed, Thalia refused to assume even an iota of guilt, and she instituted a restricted activity list that I had to abide by. Many years have passed, and the neck gaiter is the only item left from my ensemble that still fits me. As I shoveled and plowed the snow from my driveway in New Jersey, I understood why my people have been drawn to Florida like lemmings for generations: you don't have to ski, skate, shovel, or plow snow at the Fontainebleau Hotel in Miami Beach. You just have to make sure you aren't late for the buffet.

Herman es un Hijo de Puta

Part 1: No Hablo Inglés

During Christmas break of my sophomore year of college, my roommate transferred to another school. I had the entire dorm room to myself. Since I had never been known for my neatness, the room became more than a mite disheveled as the weeks progressed. (I am romanticizing my slovenly habits; the room was a mess, clothes were strewn about, the bed was never made, every drawer was ajar, and clutter threatened to overtake the room.)

At dinner one night, the Resident Assistant for our floor walked over to our table and told one of the guys, appropriately nicknamed "Derelict," that he would be getting a new roommate. Derelict's previous roommate had left one day without giving a forwarding address. (My room may have been a disaster area, but compared to Derelict's, it was the Sistine Chapel).

The RA said, "Your new roommate is from Venezuela. He doesn't speak any English. Try to clean up a bit before he gets here."

My spider-senses were tingling; my rapier-like wit was ready to spew forth. I was pondering which direction my assault should take, how long it would be before Venezuela broke off diplomatic relations with the US, renaming Derelict the "ugly American," and how long before Derelict would make a move on the burro. Then the RA dropped a bomb. "I wouldn't make any more jokes, Lentz. You're getting a Venezuelan roommate too."

It turned out that the Venezuelan government, flush with oil money, was planning to send forty students to Boston University. First they would learn English, and then they would take full university courses. I was in a state of panic and frantically pondered my options. Most of the other American students who got the news that night chose to room with another American student on the same floor. I had a choice: a Venezuelan who didn't speak any English or the Derelict. I quickly finished my dinner and went to clean my room for Paco.

As I organized the chaos that was my room, I got increasingly angry at Juan, who was going to tango in and invade my personal space. *Frigging Miguel. This is going to suck*, I thought. Eventually, I achieved a respectful semblance of order, so I went to visit my friend Nancy, who lived a few floors down. A group of people were hanging out and partying in her room. I made myself at home and launched into a tirade about the sad state of affairs I found myself in. I was at my sarcastic, snarky best.

I don't speak a word of Spanish. I only managed to get a 66 on my high school Spanish Regents exam because the teacher liked me or felt sorry for me, I'm not sure which. There was no way I would be able to communicate with Chico. I was totally screwed.

Thinking it would be funny, Nancy snuck up behind me and poured perfume down my back. I just couldn't catch a break. I dashed upstairs to take a shower before Javier got there, but when I opened the door to my room, I found Francisco already unpacking his stuff.

I smiled and nodded. Francisco did the same. I went over to shake his hand, forgetting that I smelled like a Parisian whorehouse (not that I have ever been to a Parisian whorehouse, but I imagined I probably smelled like one). When he caught a whiff of me, a quizzical expression crossed his face. I was buzzed, I didn't speak a word of Spanish, and Francisco didn't speak a word of English. How was I going to explain why I reeked of perfume?

I needed to think on my feet, but I was stoned off my ass. The best I could come up with in the moment was a dramatic wink as I slowly took off my clothes. Not my wisest decision. I put on my bathrobe and went to take a shower. When I returned, I found Francisco huddled on the corner of his bed, fully dressed, with his knees tucked to his chin. He didn't sleep at all that night, probably for fear of what his weird, scented new roommate might do to him.

The next day, I felt really bad for my foolish attempt at levity, so I went to the Foreign Language department for help. I told my story to a number of people, and while some found it very funny, others were totally appalled. Finally, an interpreter volunteered to come back to the dorm with me to explain what happened.

By the time we made it back to my room, Francisco was repacking his stuff. He was planning to sleep on the floor of Derelict's room.

The interpreter told him my story, and then they had a very long, heated conversation in Spanish that included a lot of gyrating arm motions. I stood there trying to look innocent, and finally, he smiled at me and we all shook hands.

Francisco was still convinced that I was gay, and he slept with one eye open for a few days. It took some time, but eventually he felt he could sleep facing the wall.

Part 2: Amigos!

Francisco was the de facto leader of the Venezuelans, so our room quickly became the hangout spot for his friends. To keep things fair and interesting, we made up a rule: the Venezuelans would only speak English in the room, and my friends and I would only speak Spanish. Since cursing is the universal language, that's what we all learned first.

Soon, the graffiti in the bathroom took on an international flavor:

Derelict tiene un pene pequeño

Derelict chupa verga

Herman es un hijo de puta

Derelict come mierda

It turned out that the Venezuelans weren't too fond of Derelict.

But Francisco and I shared a secret, one that eventually led to our friendship: he liked to get high. We had to be discreet because he knew that he would be sent home if he got caught. We bonded one night while smoking and watching TV. I was an insomniac and often watched until the wee hours of the morning, so Francisco had no choice but to watch too. We were both already pretty buzzed, watching an old black-and-white movie about the *Titanic*. We had made it to the point when the *Titanic* hit the iceberg and was going down. It was the most dramatic moment: passengers were running for their lives, people were jumping overboard, the ship was at a forty-five-degree angle, the giant chandelier in the dining room came crashing down, and the lower sections of the ship were filling with water.

Just then, the movie took a scheduled break and cut to a commercial for Norwegian Cruise Lines. We burst into hysterical laughter. Of course, I launched into rapid-fire comedy mode. The barbs were coming out so quickly that I could barely catch my breath, and Francisco and I both had tears running down our red faces. This became our nightly ritual. We would get high, watch TV for hours, and I would crack jokes and provide a running commentary of whatever we were watching. We spent a lot of nights cackling with laughter.

As the semester progressed, Francisco's English improved considerably. My Spanish skills, however, were *para mierda*. I was planning to transfer to SUNY Albany when the semester was over, so Francisco and I would be going our separate ways. As a way of saying adios, Francisco took me out to dinner on my last night in Boston.

We spent the evening reminiscing about the semester. I told him how much I enjoyed living with him and how thankful I was that I hadn't moved in with the Derelict. We both shuddered at the thought and unleashed a slew of Derelict jokes. Francisco brought up the night we watched the movie about the *Titanic*. I told him what a special night that had been for me, and how I felt that was the moment we became amigos.

He interrupted me and admitted that he hadn't understood a frigging word I was saying. "I knew you were trying to be funny, so I laughed. But honestly, I had no clue what you were saying. Then I did the same thing every night after that when we were watching TV, having meals, walking to class, or hanging out."

He had laughed to make me feel good. I was floored. What a selfless act of friendship. In that moment, I felt such an outpouring of emotion for Francisco. I felt so close to him.

But then Francisco looked at me, smiled, and winked. That night, I huddled on the corner of my bed, fully dressed, with my knees up to my chin. I didn't sleep a wink and even thought about going to sleep on the floor of Derelict's room.

The New Trinity

On June 27, 1981, I was standing in front of the Greenwood Manor, smoking a cigarette. With the marquee in the background, the photographer took my picture mere minutes before I would walk down the aisle and get married. The hall was packed with more than 270 people: our families, friends, coworkers, and several people who weren't invited but came anyway.

As I finished one cigarette and lit another with very unsteady hands, I reflected upon the path that got me to that moment. The journey began with adolescent Herman. My parents took me to see *Fiddler on the Roof* on Broadway. That play changed my life. No, it didn't spark a passion or love for musical theater. Instead, I was intrigued by one of the subplots that involved Chava, one of Tevye and Golde's daughters. She fell in love with a non-Jew, eloped, and was disowned by her family. My parents told me that if a Jew marries out of the faith, not only does the family disown them, but they consider them to be dead.

Not being a fan of my family, I felt like Charlie when he first spotted the Golden Ticket. I vowed then and there to marry a shiksa so my family would be forced by centuries of Jewish tradition to have nothing to do with me. There would be no -steins, -bergs, -baums, -blooms, or -blatts in my future. I sought out the Catholic school babes. This was my way out, the perfect plan. It was foolproof.

At the tender age of twenty-five, I went on vacation to Club Med Paradise Island. I was single and looking for a good time. That all changed on the second day, when I met Thalia Charitonidis. What first attracted me to her? Was it her olive skin and Mediterranean beauty? Was it her smile and sense of humor (i.e., she found me funny)? Was it the fact that there were twelve letters in her last name, including seven consonants and five vowels? While those things were certainly all appealing, what really made Thalia attractive was the fact that she was conceived in Greece, is a first-generation American, and just so happens to be Greek Orthodox. Bingo! Had she been Palestinian, just dating her would have been enough for my parents to call their attorneys, Lipshitz & Lipshitz, and Wite-Out my name from their will.

Well, after a whirlwind, six-month romance, we got engaged on Valentine's Day. In my version of the story, Thalia proposed and wanted to get married in June. I said yes, assuming it would be June of the following year. After all, it's just not possible to book a June wedding in February of the same year. I figured that a long engagement would give me time to change my mind in case I happened to meet Yasser Arafat's daughter.

Thalia agrees that we met in August and got engaged on Valentine's Day, but her recollection varies a tad. I would love to say that there was champagne, rose petals, a string quartet, and a hansom cab ride through Central Park. Instead, at a Chinese restaurant in New York City, Thalia mostly sat alone at our table, surrounded by happy couples. My nerves had gotten the best of me, and I spent the majority of the evening in the men's room. During one of my return trips to the table, I proposed, kissed her, and then immediately returned to the restroom. And yes, she planned on getting married in June of that same year. I was positive my parents would finally follow through on their threat once they learned about my engagement; they would start planning my symbolic funeral, and because I would be marrying out of the faith, it would not be catered.

Thalia had four months to book a venue and plan an entire wedding. I thought there was no way she could pull it off. It should have come as no surprise that friends of Thalia's parents owned the Greenwood Diner in Woodbridge, New Jersey. (Shocker! What are the odds that a Greek family would know someone who owns a diner?) I pictured the bridal party sitting at the diner's counter, a jukebox on every table, and the wedding cake on display by the front door, in between the lemon meringue and banana cream pies.

Unbeknownst to me, they were building a catering hall attached to the diner. If my parents somehow survived the engagement, the wedding would surely kill them. The catering hall, Greenwood Manor, was under construction and would be finished in early June. Thalia had her venue. (I should have realized that this turn of events in Thalia's favor would be a recurring theme in my life. In the years since, I have learned not to underestimate her.)

Ours would be the first wedding at Greenwood Manor, so Paul, one of the owners, asked if he could have his own photographer there to take pictures to show to potential customers. In our negotiations, I planned to relinquish final approval of all images but would demand a royalty fee for my likeness. Before I had the chance, Thalia and her parents readily agreed to Paul's request without consulting me. (I should have realized that being cut out of the decision-making process would also be a recurring theme in my life.)

As I stood there before the ceremony, I took a last drag on my cigarette and threw the butt into the parking lot. When the doors opened and I started walking down the aisle, the last few rows heard me utter, "Oh shit." After so many years, the wedding is a blur, but one memory I won't ever forget is the wedding band. It wasn't an easy task for Thalia's father to find a band that could play Greek, Jewish, and contemporary American wedding music, and he failed miserably. After much thought and deliberation, Thalia and I selected "You Make Me Feel Brand New" by The Stylistics for our first dance. It is a lovely, sentimental ballad that captured our love and devotion to each other. With the ink still drying on his green card and an extremely heavy Greek accent, the singer began, "My love, I'll never find the words, my love." Of course he couldn't find the words: they were in English! Mere words cannot explain how I felt as he killed our song. His singing "made me feel like shit."

Many years later, a woman came up to me and asked where she knew me from. I thought, *How should I know?* I was 100 percent positive that I had never met this woman before, but she was persistent and wouldn't let it go. She said that some people can never forget a face, and that she remembers mine, especially my thick, luxurious, beautiful, perfectly coiffed hair. I might be paraphrasing.

I explained to her that this happens to me often. Since she was apparently a fan of mine, I decided to figure it out with her. In some convoluted way, we uncovered the fact that she had been a waitress at the Greenwood Diner for many years. Did she work my wedding and remember me from that night? While I cut a dashing figure in my tux, I would've had to make quite an impression, so I figured that idea was farfetched. We didn't frequent the diner much after we were married, so that couldn't have been it. Just then, I lit a cigarette, and she smiled as she instantly made the connection.

I was part of the Greek Trinity.

Every Greek (redundant, I know) diner in the Northeast shares several things in common. First is a menu that defies belief in its depth and breadth. It not only encompasses breakfast, but also lunch, dinner, and late-night munchies. Perusing the menu is like riding "It's a Small World" at Disneyland, as it includes dishes from all around the globe.

Another trait shared by every Greek diner are individual portions that could feed a family of five. Customers dine in sweat-pants, and because of their girth, they can barely squeeze into the booths. On a few rare occasions, the fire department has to be called in to extricate a customer with the jaws of life.

The waitresses at every diner could be zombie extras on *The Walking Dead*. G-d only knows how they are still standing. The owner's wife or mother is permanently chained to the chair at the cash register, never allowed to leave her post.

Finally, on the wall behind the cash register, every diner has pictures of the celebrities who have been patrons of the diner. Minor celebrities and local politicians are positioned around the perimeter, and as the fame of the celebrity increases, their photo is given a spot closer to the center. The center is sacred ground, the source of great pride for each diner, the cause célèbre, the Greek Hall of Fame.

Like every other diner, the Greenwood Manor had their own version of the Greek Trinity. Above the owner's wife or mother were autographed pictures of Telly Savalas, Greek actor from the hit TV show *Kojak*, and Ernie Anastos, Greek TV news anchor and tri-state area icon. Squarely in the center, rounding out the Trinity, was a picture of yours truly, Herman "The Long Island Jew" Lentz, smoking a cigarette in front of the Greenwood Manor marquee.

Open twenty-four hours a day, seven days a week for the past ten years, every customer who passed by the cash register would recognize a smiling Telly, and they certainly knew Ernie from the nightly news. But who was that mysterious, debonair man in the middle with the great head of hair, wearing a tuxedo, and smoking a cigarette in front of the marquee? Was he a famous actor from the old country (Greece, not New York)? Also, why hadn't he written a note to Paul, or at a minimum, autographed his picture? (The single vowel in my last name would have given away the fact that I am not Greek.) I imagine my picture was a source of great bewilderment to all.

So we finally figured out how that woman knew me. For years, she, along with countless others, had gazed at my photo and understandably fantasized about me. Had I been carrying any eight-by-ten headshots, I would have given her one, complete with autograph. (Delusions of grandeur have also been a recurring theme in my life.)

After Thalia and I were married, I emigrated from New York to Jersey. I literally and figuratively put two bridges between me and my past. What I didn't know at the time was how strong the bonds of la famiglia are in Greek culture, or that Thalia and her family were ardent disciples of that principle, even going so far as to welcome my family into the mix.

Instead of sitting shiva and casting me and my shiksa bride out, my parents embraced Thalia and her family. Much to my horror, they invited Thalia's parents to every Passover and Rosh Hashanah, and my parents were included in every Greek Easter and Christmas. Pot roast became a staple at Thalia's family dinners. When everyone got together yet again for Thanksgiving, we celebrated the pilgrims' first harvest with traditional Thanksgiving dishes: moussaka and pastitsio. Had I known that my *Fiddler* plot would have backfired, I would have married a Jewess. Jewish in-laws rarely get along, and unlike Thalia's family, they aren't as likely to spit on me in the name of good luck.

Gummies

What do you do when you can't smoke pot anymore? These days, the thought of taking a bong hit would give both me and my cardiologist a heart attack. With a decent toke off a joint, I start coughing up pieces of my lungs. The other problem is that weed stinks, literally, not figuratively. Pot smells like two skunks engaging in angry sex. If I wanted to puff on the magic dragon, I would be worried that the police, my parents, or Thalia would bust me.

So, without telling Thalia, I decided to try weed-infused gummy bears.

Gummies are cute, innocent, and harmless looking. They brought me back to my childhood, when the only adverse effect of eating too many gummies would be a bad tummy ache and a lecture from my dentist at my next checkup. I was warned not to take more than two, and that they would take roughly forty-five minutes to take effect. So, with the clock ticking, my relaxing evening began.

But then I panicked: I had forgotten about Thalia. It was a Friday night and we weren't going out, so it was TV night at the Lentzes'. One of the few responsibilities that Thalia has bestowed upon me is being in charge of nighttime entertainment. While some might not think this is an arduous task, Thalia's viewing preferences are very particular. It's hard to find something to watch that ticks all the boxes. She does not like anything suspenseful, scary, anything with too much drama, any pain or suffering, competition of any sort, lowbrow comedy, people not being nice to each other, deceit, intrigue, reruns, or any athletic event. The list goes on and on.

Unbeknownst to me, she had a habit of scurrying to the bathroom to avoid seeing objectionable material. For the longest time, I thought she had a recurring urinary tract infection and was too embarrassed to discuss it. Being the compassionate, caring person that I am, I would pause the show and wait patiently for her to return so she wouldn't miss anything. This would only prompt an immediate return trip to the bathroom. When my searches proved futile, I have spent many a catatonic night watching *Property Brothers*, *Love It or List It,* or an assortment of cooking shows.

On this particular night, my exhaustive search yielded a win for the kid. I found a romantic comedy that was streaming on demand. After watching the trailer, Thalia signed off on it. I sighed in contentment. As the movie began, Grace Slick was softly singing in my head: "One pill makes you happy..." I was planning for an evening of being stoned, and if Thalia didn't have a UTI, there was no telling how the night might end.

Right off the bat, we encountered a small problem: the movie was in Spanish. I could have sworn it was an English-language film, so I knew something had to be wrong. With my grasp on reality fading fast, I started frantically pressing every button on the remote control. Nothing worked. My fingers were dancing, and I was scanning, scrolling, and toggling the up arrow, down, right, left, and every combination of buttons I could imagine. Despite my best efforts, "el movieo no habla inglés."

So, me being me, I gave up. I told Thalia to just forget it, it's not working, no mas, we will watch something else. Thalia insisted that I call Verizon customer service and make them fix it. *She actually wants me to deal with something? Doesn't she know better after all these years of marriage?* The hair, the genius that is my sense of humor, the silky-soft skin—I bring so much to the table, but dealing with things is not a talking point on my resume. I abdicated decision-making and all responsibility to her early in our marriage, and Thalia gladly accepted that mantle.

I bitterly protested, saying that I was willing to eat the $5.99 rental fee (I had rented the movie in HD for the additional $1), but Thalia was adamant. I mentioned all the money we waste on simultaneous Netflix, Apple TV+, Amazon Prime, and Hulu subscriptions. What's another six bucks?

Nevertheless, she was steadfast. To her, it was the principle of the thing. I pulled my wallet off the nightstand and started throwing random bills on the bed. Not my finest moment. I was putting my foot down. There was absolutely no way I was going to call Verizon customer service.

Five minutes later, I was screaming into the phone, "OPERATOR. OPERATOR!" Trying to navigate every prompt that Verizon has designed to foil a rational person was totally screwing with me as I stood at the gates of Gummy Land. Finally, just as I was ready to throw my phone out the window, I got a real human on the other end of the line. She had me enter a sequence of codes that did not fix my TV but could potentially launch our nation's nuclear arsenal. Eventually, she put me on hold to do some additional research.

With pleading eyes (if my eyes were visible at the time, they would have been pleading), I looked at Thalia. *Please, please, please! Haven't I done enough? I'll even watch Episode 2 of Project Runway Children's Edition Season 1 just to make this end.*

No, she said. It was this movie. Period.

Finally, the Verizon lady came back on the line. Through hysterical fits of laughter, she told me that the first seven minutes of the movie were in Spanish and then it changes to English.

"Tu madre! El televisionieo es bueno? El movieo es un español, then changes to English? You're fucking kidding me. This is mierda de bull!"

I was officially gummied and all sense of logic and perspective had fallen sloppy dead. I wasn't sure if Thalia realized I was buzzed, but she might have had an inkling when I attacked an industrial-size Costco bag of potato chips like it was an individual snack pack, along with a tub o' salsa.

We made it through the movie without any further trouble. For all I knew, the entire movie could have been in Spanish, but I didn't care. Thalia fell asleep, but I was still one toke over the line. An episode of *The Big Bang Theory* started playing. In my head, I heard, "Sheldon turns to Penny and smiles." On the screen, Sheldon turned to Penny and smiled! After a little conversation, I heard, "Leonard enters the room." And guess what? Leonard entered the room!

And then it hit me: my mother was right! I am special, I am clairvoyant.

For the next hour, I tested it out and discovered that I knew what was going to happen on the show before it actually happened. I wondered, *How can I use these powers for evil instead of good?* My mind was racing with the endless possibilities and I couldn't sleep.

The following morning, I woke up with a groggy head. The sheets on my side of the bed were littered with potato chip crumbles and salsa drippings, and I had a really bad tummy ache. *I guess I overdid it.*

Thalia woke up and switched on the television. "What's up with the TV?" she asked. She could hear it too!

This is unbelievable, I thought. *I have the ability to share my powers with others!*

And then reality set in. Stan Lee is not going to base a new superhero on me; something was up. Despite the fact that I thought I had already fulfilled my quota of fixing stuff for the year, Thalia ordered me to get the TV working right.

After another call to Verizon, I found out that while smashing buttons on the remote control, I had somehow activated a little-known feature called Descriptive Video Service, designed to help visually impaired and blind people enjoy television by narrating the action on screen.

Herman smiles, stops typing, and gets up from the computer.

El Finale

(The End)

The Worm Has Turned

After being friends with Jim and Andre for over twenty years, I thought I'd heard it all. There was nothing Jim could say that would shock me anymore. Or so I thought.

Jim and Andre are longtime friends of Thalia's. When she introduced us, Jim instantly saw me as a straight man who had led a very sheltered life growing up on the streets of Long Island. In other words, to Jim, a gay man, I was prey. Right from the start, Jim would say and do things with the sole intent of embarrassing me. He would freely share—in vivid detail—stories from his early days in New York City in the eighties and his "extremely active" participation in the gay sexual revolution.

I first met Jim and Andre at a birthday party at Posh, a gay bar in the city. I have to admit that I was nervous and didn't know what to expect. I was young and in my prime, with a great head of hair and a sparkle in my eye. In a gay bar, I was USDA Grade A Prime beef. If not for the fact that I have no flair for style, despise shopping, and don't know the lyrics to any show tunes, I would have been too irresistible. I feared that I would be kidnapped, sold into a life of slavery in an Arab sheik's harem, and be called Hisman instead of Herman.

Much to my relief, no one hit on me that night. As I reflect on that evening now, I feel kind of insulted. In a bar packed with drunken gay guys, not one had the courage to approach me? What was that all about? Maybe it was the prettiest-girl-at-the-dance syndrome, or perhaps the fact that I held Thalia's arm in a vice-like death grip that turned off any prospective suitors.

I did finally release Thalia long enough to go to the bathroom. Hanging on the men's room door was a sign that read, "Limit one person at a time." I thought, *Why do they even have this sign? It must be a very small bathroom.* I was quite naive. It took me a couple of seconds to put two and two together, or in this case, one and one together. Unless the participants were acrobats, multiple occupancy wasn't physically possible in that tiny lavatory.

A few years later, gay marriage became legal and we proudly attended Jim and Andre's wedding. It was a special day and everything was positively perfect. Despite the fact that I was in the minority as a heterosexual man, once again, unbelievably, no one hit on me. I hadn't even been surgically attached to Thalia that time. What gives?

Toward the end of the affair, nature called. Just as I rounded the corner to the men's room, I heard the door close. There was no sign on the door limiting the occupancy to one person, but I didn't think my wait would be long. Moments later, it sounded like they were filming a porno in there. They were really going at it. Despite how far I have come over the years in my open-mindedness, I kept saying to myself, "Don't think about what's going on in there. Just don't think about what's going on in there." While I applauded the stamina of the participants, and from the sounds of it, the multitude of positions that were being attempted, I really needed to use the bathroom. I just kept repeating my mantra: "Don't think about what's going on in there."

Finally, the door opened and two very attractive women walked out. I sighed and said, "Think about what was going on in there, really *really* think about what was going on in there!"

So, after twenty years, I have become immune to Jim's antics. His goal has always been to shock me, and in the beginning, it was very easy. The longer we've been friends, the harder it has gotten to surprise me. I figured that the worm has finally turned.

Recently, the four of us went out to dinner. Andre vigorously shook his head, trying to silence his husband, but Jim decided to tell us about a gay strip club in Mexico where the male strippers serve tequila foreskin shots for a dollar. Had my ears deceived me? While contemplating this act, I winced and then shook my head in disgust. This was too much to swallow.

It was hard for me to imagine such a thing. I had that part of my anatomy removed when I was eight days old at a celebration, surrounded by family and friends with their mouths full of bagels and lox and schmear, all yelling "Mazel Tov!" I've never seen one with a hoodie.

I was still trying to figure out the logistics of a foreskin shot when Jim, realizing my distress, described the lurid process in great detail and with immense glee. I tried to catch the waitress's attention to cancel my order of sausage and peppers; I'd lost my appetite. I thought about the poor Jewish stripper at that club, and how he had to do the strip club's books during the day because he couldn't make his ends meet.

I thought I had come a long way, baby, but Jim still has the ability to blow my mind. Despite his best efforts, my mind is the only thing he has had the opportunity to blow.

Minority Groups

It was 1973, and I was in my freshman year at Boston University. I took what was referred to as a gut course: a class that required a minimal amount of effort. Minority Groups 101 had three required books you didn't have to read, and midterm and final exams you didn't have to take. All that was truly required was a class presentation on a minority group that lives in Boston. It was practically the perfect course. My roommate Smitty and I giddily signed up.

Our attendance was sporadic at best. As the semester progressed, other groups signed up to do their presentations on Irish, Jewish, Polish, and Italian people living in Boston. On one of the rare occasions we actually showed up to class, the professor announced a list of students who would be presenting that Thursday. Lentz and Smith were part of the lineup. Needless to say, we had done nothing to date.

I'm not proud to admit it, but even in my classes with more stringent requirements, I only completed the minimum amount of work. I led a very Cheech and Chong lifestyle. Smitty and I were both New Yorkers, where the Rockefeller drug laws made possession of a joint a criminal offense with a mandatory jail sentence. Marijuana was also illegal in Massachusetts, but in the dorms at Boston University, it was tolerated. Everyone just looked the other way. In fact, dealers would roam the dorm hallways and knock on every door to promote the specials of the week. I wanted to study, but at fifteen dollars for an ounce of Mexican weed and thirty dollars for an ounce of Columbian, as an accounting major with a minor in economics, I did the math and the deals were just too good to pass up.

With no other options, Smitty and I sprang into action. We headed straight to the registrar to drop the class. As it turned out, the deadline to drop the course was Friday, one day after our presentation. *Nothing to lose! Might as well take a crack at it*, I thought. Later that night, we brainstormed in a room full of smoke, which was probably not the most productive atmosphere for dealing with a major problem. Smitty and I debated our options. In the span of a day and a half, we had to pick a minority group, do the research, and write an entire paper. What minority groups were even left? All the best ones were already taken. We were stuck with choosing from the minority of minority groups.

When the smoke had cleared and reality set in, we went back to our dorm. Sitting on his bed, Smitty spewed a constant stream of "shit" and "fuck." For variety, he threw in the occasional "My mother will kill me." His panic was not helping my creative process.

I berated myself for my writer's block. "Come on, H. You can do this! You're resourceful, you can figure this out. All you need is an angle, a random thought, an inkling, just one small spark to set it all in motion." That became my mantra: "Just one small spark." I repeated it over and over as I pounded my fists against my head.

And then it came to me.

As Smitty lay on his bed in the fetal position, I sat at my desk and started writing. After careful consideration, I decided not to tell Smitty what I was up to. I was already concerned that I might have to take him to the university counseling center, and I knew that my idea would send him there for at least a few days.

On Thursday, the day of the big presentation, I led a semi-catatonic Smitty to class. I told him I'd written a report on a minority group in Boston. "We're going to be fine, Smitty. Don't worry, I've got this. You trust me, don't you?"

He had a moment of clear-headed lucidity, turned to glare at me, and said, "Fuck no."

It was too late to turn back, so the show must go on. We were the last group to present that day.

Lights, camera, action! Ladies and gentlemen, we're proud to present an HL Production. Here we go!

The first thing I did was thank all the groups who presented before us, saying how informative and entertaining their presentations had been. I took Suck-Up 101 during my first semester.

Just then, my conscience got the better of me. *What the fuck am I doing? This is totally absurd! They're going to boo us out of class.*

With no choice but to proceed, and with the drop/add safety net a day away, I cleared my throat and began. *"We'd like to discuss a minority group that has been immigrating into Boston twice as fast as any other group. They buy a single train ticket, but then two of them sit in the seat. That's right, folks, today we're talking about the influx of midgets into Boston."*

(Author's Note: I realize how politically incorrect my comments were, but it was 1973. I have evolved a little in the years since.)

The class was silent. You could've heard a pin drop. Predictably, Smitty's knees buckled. He was down for the count. All of my bodily fluids were ready to drain from every orifice. Have you ever heard the advice that you should picture your audience in their underwear if you're nervous? Well, on that day, the opposite was true: I pictured myself standing there totally naked. Not only was I naked, but I was totally emasculated as if I had just emerged from the Charles River on a cold winter's day.

And then, from the back of the classroom, the professor burst out laughing. The masses followed. My confidence was surging, and as each joke landed, I was still naked but ready for a porn scene without the assistance of a fluffer.

I did a bold, ten-minute monologue on the trials and tribulations of little people. I explained that midgets were frustrated by the height of urinals in public restrooms, shopping for clothing, and being used as an armrest by tall people. I made every cheap joke I could think of. I also tried to be empathetic and encourage some compassion for my minority group when I described "the sad expression on their faces at Disney Land when they can only enjoy the rides intended for toddlers."

"Their only alternative is to turn to a life of crime. Robbing banks is problematic since the tellers can't see them when they approach the counter. Instead, they've been reduced to stealing the tags from the bottom of chairs and sofas that say, 'Do not remove under penalty of law.'"

I explained that the Boston Police Department was growing frustrated because they couldn't find the culprits. It seems that the midgets would hide between the policemen's legs. *"If the cops would bother looking between their own legs instead of busting kids for pot, Boston would be a better place to live."*

The room erupted in thunderous applause as the class leaped to their feet for a standing ovation. Smitty punched my arm and then gave me a reluctant hug. After my genius performance, I expected to receive an A in the course. It would have been a boost to my anemic GPA.

I forgot the class was pass/fail.

We passed.

The next semester, Smitty transferred to SUNY Binghamton. I would like to think he became a carny. While I was very relieved to have survived the course, I knew I had to start working on our presentation for our African Studies class.

Hakuna Matata.

Hair Today, (Hopefully) Gone Tomorrow

People have been asking me if I will write a story about my experiences during the pandemic. As I think of all the lives that have been lost, unemployment rates skyrocketing, Americans waiting in line for food, and the uncertainty of what the future will bring, I believe it would be insensitive of me to write something amusing about our shared difficult experience. Also, I don't want to start a new story until I finish my rom-com about the Holocaust.

But seriously, I need to find a topic worthy of my talents. Countless poignant and touching tales are being told about people's experiences during this crisis. What could I possibly add? I'm sure that some readers would enjoy hearing about my adventures in quarantine with Thalia. Since I hope to keep both halves of my assets, I don't think that is a good idea. I had decided not to be topical and entertain you with stories from my past. That is, until the crisis finally hit home.

One morning, as I performed my daily hair ritual, I noticed that my hair was getting long. To my horror, I was developing side curls and was beginning to look like a Hasidic Jew. As I gazed into the mirror at my once perfectly coiffed hair, the envy of all, a Herman Ch-ch-ch-chia Pet was staring back at me.

I felt hideous. I started wearing hoodies around the house to hide the mess on my head. When I needed to go out for essentials, I went out of my way to shop at stores where they wouldn't recognize me. It was a dark time. Unsurprisingly, Thalia took glee in my dilemma. She started talking about a man bun. When I rejected that idea, she offered to cut my hair. I love Thalia and trust her with my life, but I do not trust her with my hair.

I'd like to apologize in advance to the follicly challenged for the rest of this story. I realize that my feelings about my hair border on obsession. Although I cannot carry a tune (I mouth the words to "Happy Birthday"), can't draw a straight line, and have no musical talent at all, the Big Guy gave me a great head of hair to make up for all of those shortcomings. If further proof of divine intervention is required, you'll be delighted to hear that I have a minor cowlick, which makes my hair just short of flawless, as nothing can or should be perfect. That cowlick keeps me semi-humble.

Normally, I have my hair cut every five to five and a half weeks, depending on the growing season. Thanks to lockdowns, I found myself seven weeks overdue. I was beginning to feel like Lawrence Talbot when the full moon appears. Early in the pandemic, when there was a mad rush at the stores, people were panic buying toilet paper, soap, disinfectant, and bread. The shelves were bare and hoarding became the norm. I must admit that I got caught up in the madness and rushed to the store to buy hair products before they ran out. I couldn't believe they weren't limiting the sale to two products per family.

Despite all the loving care and constant attention that I have given my hair, genetics surely played a major role in my magnificent mane. I don't know who I got this glorious hair from, but it certainly wasn't either of my parents. My father was bald, and my mother had thinning hair. (Had there been DNA tests back then, so many questions would have been answered and possibly some of my issues resolved.)

My vanity goes way back. Back in the '70s, long hair was the style, and I flaunted mine. I wore it parted in the center, shoulder length, shagged, and layered. I would never put it in a ponytail, as I thought that was the lazy way out. Besides, it would be unfair to the viewing public. I did pay the price: I had to get up half an hour earlier for prep time. However, people would occasionally stop me on the street to comment on it, so it was all worth it.

So when I found myself in the new world of social distancing, unsure when things would get back to normal, I started putting more and more product into my hair to get some semblance of order. I was in desperate need of a cut. I needed my stylist, I needed my Sheri. Now, I consider Sheri to be an essential worker, but much to my dismay, the State of New Jersey did not.

My relationship with Sheri began fourteen years ago. After a series of subpar performances, my stylist at the time just wasn't cutting it for me anymore. I knew I had to find someone new, but I didn't know where to begin. I went to a local salon and asked to speak to the owner. When I asked which stylist was the best in the shop, she said she was. As we were dealing with my hair, the genesis of my vanity, I offered to pay her for a consultation. I needed to make sure she was The One. Whether she was intrigued or it was just a slow day, she indulged me.

Following my passionate sermon about the history of my hair and my infatuation with it, and a question-and-answer session about her professional experience, I let her brush it and make some suggestions. Though I was pleased that she noticed my minor cowlick, I was still apprehensive and unsure if our relationship would progress to the next level.

Then she said the seven words I'd been waiting to hear: "You have a great head of hair." Sheri and I have collaborated on my hair ever since; I provide the canvas upon which Sheri performs her artistry. Over the years, my style has changed. As I more than gracefully age, my hair has gone from a lush brown to a distinguished, silvery gray. The distinguished, silvery gray hairs are coarser, and have necessitated a change from a center part to a part on the right, and then a few years later, a part on the left. Each change was made only after a number of heated discussions and a few sketches.

Sheri is totally on board with my insanity, and in fact, she is a co-conspirator. Either she is a true believer in the power of my coiffure or I am a lavish tipper, and while I believe the former, the latter is also true. She does face quite a quandary where I am concerned: what time is best to schedule my appointments? If I am the first appointment of the morning, everything is downhill after that. If I am the last appointment of the day, while she goes home on a high, the day-long anticipation must be unbearable. In addition, she knows she has to be at the top of her game, and G-d only knows where her hands have been during the course of the day. Ultimately, we reached a compromise: I will alternate between the first and the last appointment. (The middle of the day doesn't work for me, as it could affect my tee times.)

I've only had one incident with Sheri, a bad haircut in the fall of 2012. I immediately put Sheri on probation. She realized the error of her ways, cited a medical condition, and the next cut was gratis. Things improved dramatically, and we put the unpleasantness behind us. But then, a few months ago, Sheri made a major faux pas. I started growing a beard. It was coming in nicely, and I was keeping it closely cropped and manicured. I was hoping for more pepper than salt, but unfortunately, that was not the case. As I was lamenting this fact to Sheri, she mentioned that she is an expert at coloring and could easily fix it.

I couldn't believe what I was hearing, especially from Sheri. Blasphemy! I angrily told her to put down her scissors, turn my chair around, and listen to me. I said, "Sheri, I am a purist, and I have been blessed. If I cheat on my beard and get caught, people will question my hair. It would ruin me. Why would I risk it?"

She apologized and cited another medical condition. Her health problems concerned me, partly because I hoped she was okay, but mainly because finding a new stylist meant interviews, checking references, and reviewing work samples. That was too daunting a task, so I gave her a pass.

And then the pandemic hit. After twelve long weeks, I was getting desperate. Despite her words of comfort over the phone, the best that Sheri could do was to tell me to hang in there until her shop could reopen. In the interim, Thalia's hairdresser made a house call, and when she finished Thalia, she offered to cut my hair. The situation was dire. It had been a long time. I really needed it. Sheri wasn't around. I'm just a man and I have needs, so I reluctantly agreed.

As fate would have it, Sheri called not long after to say that she would be opening the shop on a limited basis. She wanted me to come in right away. Oy vey. I made some excuse about being exposed to the virus, but I promised to come in as soon as possible. I stalled as long as I could, and I even scheduled an appointment with every intention of not showing up, all the while coaxing my hair to grow faster.

Eventually, I had to face the music. I sat in her chair and she ran her fingers through my hair, then a brush. With dramatic flair, she spun the chair around and said, "You have been cheating on me!"

I pleaded, "Sheri, please! It was a one-time thing! It meant nothing to me and will never happen again." I even tried citing a medical condition. Would she ever trust me again? For that matter, should I trust her? She has scissors, after all; she could pull a Lorena Bobbitt on my hair. Needless to say, the relationship was strained for a while.

How does Thalia deal with me? (Specifically, my obsession with my hair, for according to Thalia, I have multiple issues that she has to deal with.) For the most part, she ignores my vanity. If she gets really annoyed with me, she tells me I am getting a bald spot on the back of my head. (Thank you, dear reader, I agree. That is unnecessarily cruel and messed up.) I run into the bathroom, and like a dog chasing its tail, I twirl around trying to see the back of my head in the mirror. Then I schedule an earlier appointment with Sheri to make sure everything is kosher.

My sons have inherited my sense of humor, but sadly, they have not been blessed with my hair genes. Although I love them more than anything and would give them a kidney, a lung, or part of my liver without a second's thought, hair plugs? NEVER.

Some of you may think I am joking or exaggerating. I'm not.

All I can say is:

> Hair, hair, hair, hair,
>
> Flow it, show it
>
> Long as I can grow it
>
> My hair!

It Started off with a Colonoscopy

A few years ago, one of my closest friends, Dennis, told me that he was going in for a colonoscopy. As a recent survivor of the procedure, I recommended that he purchase a hefty amount of Preparation H wipes with aloe, install a TV in his bathroom, and if that wasn't possible, get a good book or some magazines. Most importantly, I advised him not to wipe but to dab gently.

As the extremely proud father of a doctor (excuse me, a *surgeon*), I have witnessed the rigorous education firsthand: four years of undergrad, studying for the MCATs, four years of medical school, five years of residency, and a one-year fellowship to finally become a surgeon. After all that training and sacrifice, this poor gastroenterologist will have the pleasure of staring at Dennis's hairy, pimply butt.

When the day of the colonoscopy finally arrived, Dennis was a good five pounds lighter after a night of prepping for the procedure. Like Captain James T. Kirk, this doctor was about to boldly go where no man had gone before. However, as they were doing the pre-op testing, the doctor grew concerned that Dennis's heartbeat had the pulsating rhythm of a rap group on crystal meth. Alarmed, the doctor canceled the colonoscopy and sent Dennis for an urgent cardiac catheterization to check for a blockage in his arteries.

Unbeknownst to his doctors, Dennis had a problem with condiments since childhood. Schmears of cream cheese became the gateway to mounds of Russian dressing, egg rolls drowning in Dai Day duck sauce, and glasses with U-Bet chocolate syrup dripping down the sides. His mother's mantra, "eat, tateleh," perpetually rang in his ears. We all should have picked up on the telltale signs. If one only looked closely enough and connected the dots, it was obvious that Dennis had issues: the chipmunk cheeks, the husky wardrobe, the food stains littering his clothing.

When the catheter could not penetrate the layers of cream cheese that congested his blood vessels, the doctors had no option but to perform not a single, not a double, but a *triple* bypass surgery.

The surgery was a success. Dennis was fine.

About a week later, the shit hit the fan. He was admitted to the ICU with low blood pressure, fever, and difficulty breathing. His organs were not functioning properly and he was septic. It was extremely serious. We rushed to the hospital and joined Dennis's friends and family in the packed waiting room. Everyone was freaking out about how critical Dennis's condition was. Finally, we were allowed to see him in small groups for short visits. When we walked into his ICU room, I saw him lying in bed, hooked up to a respirator. I glanced down to compose myself. *I can't look, it's too hard,* I thought. *It just hurts so much to think of anything happening to him.*

I gathered myself, realizing I had to be strong. I was there to show my support. I was there for Dennis. I love him and I wanted him to know how much he means to all of us. Finally, I looked at him. Hooked up to countless monitors and contraptions, he looked like hell. It broke my heart to see him that way, and I struggled to swallow the big lump in my throat.

But then, I noticed that his hospital gown was open and pulled up to his waist. There were four to six other people in the room; didn't anyone else notice that we were staring at full-frontal Dennis? In hushed tones, the others were saying that he looked good. That certainly wasn't true from my angle. I suddenly felt sorry for Lee, Dennis's wife, his current condition not the only reason for my sympathy.

Hooked up to machines, having your gallbladder removed in an emergency surgery, and being pumped full of meds would make anyone look like shit. On top of that, Dennis is exceptionally hairy; actually, he looks like he is covered in fur. (He once participated in a Hairy Man Contest on a cruise and came in second. Sasquatch came in third.) To make matters worse, the nurses had to shave major sections of Dennis's body to prep him for surgery. His torso looked like a tropical rain forest that had been ravaged by land developers and loggers. I thought of the saying, "You can't see the forest for the trees." In Dennis's case, with his legs spread apart, you could see both the forest and a sapling, along with a couple of pebbles.

Just then, I noticed that "it" was staring at me no matter where I went, like Mona Lisa's eyes. Thinking like a true friend, I said, "It's a little cold in here. Maybe we should cover Dennis up." My plea fell on deaf ears. I could almost hear it talking to me, saying, "Be a brother, how about a little cover?" I was unnerved. *Why is it staring at me?* As I waited for my turn to talk to Dennis, I decided that I just had to do something. I was seeing a side of Dennis that I'd never seen before and hoped to never see again.

Finally, it was my turn. I approached his bed, leaned over to whisper in his ear, and discreetly tried to pull down his hospital gown. Unfortunately, he was lying on it and it wouldn't budge. I tugged harder, but it was no use. I was afraid that if I pulled too hard, I would disconnect him from his machines. I needed more leverage, but I really didn't want to get any closer to what was going on down there. Alas, Dennis's modesty would have to remain unprotected.

"Sorry, little fella, I can't help you out."

We went back to the waiting room. I must have looked really distressed because everyone kept asking me how Dennis looked. What could I say? "He looked so . . . small in that big hospital bed." Or, "They are keeping his room very cold. It must be because of his fever." Maybe I should have said, "I would not recommend letting your children see him in his current condition." I asked the others who had been in the room with us if they noticed anything revealing about Dennis, but no one mentioned it.

Thank G-d, Dennis made a full recovery. It's like it never happened. Unfortunately, after that whole ordeal, Dennis still had to go for a colonoscopy. As for me, I now suffer from PTDD: Post-Traumatic Dennis Disorder.

On a final note, I recently went for an eye exam, and I was diagnosed with macropsia, a neurological condition affecting my visual perception, in which objects appear larger than they actually are.

Lights, Camera, Action!

I recently celebrated the birth of my fifth grandchild, and it brought back a flood of memories. When Thalia was pregnant, we enrolled in Lamaze class. That first class came close to being my last. As each couple introduced themselves and said why they were there, a few henpecked husbands mentioned something about wanting to share in the miracle of birth. The majority of the guys, however, pointed to their wives and made a snide comment about being forced to attend.

When it was our turn, I just couldn't help myself. I gotta be me, after all. I said, "I hope that this is more like a Le Mans class. Maybe the baby will speed right out!" I was on a roll. After the laughter subsided, I said, "Seriously, I am here because, to quote Prissy from *Gone with the Wind*, 'I don't know nothin bout birthin babies.'" Tough crowd. I should have quit at the Le Mans line.

I was attentive and took copious notes. I was going to be such a good birthing partner that they'd surely name a wing of the hospital after me. Everything was going fine until the instructor showed the film of an actual birth. Not a fan of the horror film genre, I was freaked out. At the end of the film, I expected a team from *CSI* to seal the delivery room with crime scene tape.

When it was time for the real thing, the actual birth turned out to be even worse. When Thalia was fully dilated and breathing through her contractions, a nurse said, "Doctor, we're about to lose one!" They escorted me to a chair in the far corner of the delivery room and left me to tend to my wife. Periodically, between Thalia's screams, they would check on me to make sure I was okay. I appreciated their attention, but they ignored my request for some ginger ale and saltines.

Despite the fact that Thalia got considerably more attention than I did, we both survived the birth. When the doctor asked if I wanted to come over and meet my baby, I made sure to wait until after the hazmat team had cleaned up the area and the kid was showered and dressed.

Despite that rocky start, parenting was a great adventure. Then, on April 17, 2016, Thalia and I were sitting in a hospital awaiting the birth of our first grandchild. I thought, *I'm going to be a grandfather. The circle of life continues*. It was a big responsibility that I took very seriously. I felt immense pressure when I realized that I had fewer than six months to come up with a new theme for my annual holiday card that would include the newest bundle of joy. As I racked my brain, I finally came up with a line that I really liked: "Eight Lentzes a-Leaping." Unfortunately, even with the new baby, there would only be seven Lentzes. Was there any possibility of another baby hiding in there? My daughter-in-law did get pretty big.

In the end, there was only one baby, and she was perfect. As soon as I saw her, my cell phone was out, and it was a constant stream of pictures. She was asleep, tied up in her swaddle, peaceful and still, and I was clicking away like a madman. It was the same picture over and over again, but I didn't care. As each person picked up the baby for the first time, I took multiple pictures from every angle.

Some might say that it's natural for a grandparent to want to capture those first moments, and that there is nothing wrong with it. I am embarrassed to admit that things only got progressively worse. As Leila was sleeping in her bassinette and I was developing a blister on my thumb, the nurse walked in to change the baby's first diaper. First diaper! This is the stuff that precious memories are made of!

I remembered a Pampers commercial from around the time Jimmy and Jonathon were infants that claimed the average baby will use 6,896 diapers before they are potty trained. Wanting to keep track of how many diapers we still had to go, I made a note every time it was changed. I had the opportunity to film the first in a long series of 6,896 poops, or possibly less as she is a Lentz and would be anything but average. I was going to capture the moment.

I switched to video mode to film *The Changing of the First Diaper*. In the blink of an eye, I turned into Herman Spielberg. I was going in for close-ups, panning the crowd for reaction shots, and thinking about what I was going to do in post-production. I considered the lighting, camera angles, and the use of filters. I dared to dream big. Should I license a song or hire a composer to score an original soundtrack? Could I get an Academy Award winner to make a cameo in a future production?

Suddenly, I thought, *What the hell am I doing? Am I really filming the changing of a diaper? What is wrong with me?* I didn't stop, but at least I thought about it.

And then, as the nurse unsnapped the diaper, I moved in for the money shot. I expected the nurse to hold it up in the air so we could all marvel at the first poop. I was ready to capture the oohs and aahs of the crowd. To my dismay, she went off script, and for some unexplained reason, she did not display it. She just folded it over, put it to the side, picked up Leila's legs, and wiped her tuchus. I was pissed. *What the hell is Nurse Ratched doing? This is my big moment!* I felt like yelling, "Cut!" We needed to do a second take, and I would make it look seamless in the editing phase. "Leila, sweetheart, Bubala, you think you can give me another poop?"

That night, as I was watching and rewatching *The Changing of the First Diaper*, it hit me: what was I going to do with this video? Is there anyone out there who actually wants to see what is, in my mind, a monumental event? But in the scheme of things, is it really that bad? After all, people film all sorts of things. For example, some people film the actual birth, which is a video I would never want to see. Who would you possibly show that video to? Watching someone else's wedding video is bad enough, especially if you were there, but a birth? No way. People film a bris, which is another video I would take a pass on watching. Introducing circumcision to the world is probably one of the underlying reasons for the rampant antisemitism. Some people even film the conception, although they might just think they're making a sex tape. I could be talked into watching that, depending on the couple.

So, I was faced with a dilemma. What should I do with my video? There will be no need to play it at her first birthday party; they can see her diaper being changed in real time. I suppose I could screen it at her Sweet Sixteen or show it to her prom date, but it would be pretty much guaranteed that she'd never speak to me again. What about at her engagement party? I could sneak it into the loop of pictures that plays in the background. But if she gets engaged in her twenties, I will be in my eighties. Fair play would dictate that she would show a picture of me and my first soiled Depends at my funeral.

Ultimately, I realized that it was a shitty idea. So that night, I gave Leila her first present from her grandfather: I deleted the video.

Finding a New Doctor

While I still have a sparkle in my eyes and an impish grin, I also have to acknowledge that I'm not a kid anymore. At the time of writing, I am sixty-six years old; concerns over my health have taken on more significance as I've aged. To that end, I'm diligent about going for my annual physical. Unfortunately, my doctor of many years recently retired, and I was forced to find a new doc. This was an extremely important decision, so what criteria should I use in this search?

I prepared a list to help me weigh all the various factors. Are they in network? How extensive is their training? What is their hospital affiliation? How many years of experience do they have? The list of considerations went on and on: location, bedside manner, personality, sense of humor (i.e., finding me funny). Since my yearly physical now includes the dreaded prostate exam, I ultimately decided that the most crucial determiner would be the size of the doctor's hands.

I figured that a petite female doctor or maybe an Asian doctor would fit the bill nicely.

Unfortunately, selecting a new doctor is not like going on JDate. There were no pictures, profiles, or glove sizes, so I made my selection based solely on sex and last name. After waiting weeks for the first available appointment, I finally met my new doctor, the ideal caregiver for my needs: an Asian woman.

The office was nearby, the doctor's schooling was respectable, and the receptionist was young and pretty (not part of my criteria, but it didn't hurt), so things were looking promising. Viagra commercials advise that if you have an erection lasting more than four hours after taking the little blue pill, you should see a doctor immediately. Well, this must have been the doctor that Pfizer Pharmaceuticals had in mind, as one look at my new physician could make any erection dissipate immediately. She was a rotund, older woman with hairs growing out of the assorted moles on her face. They say there's a lid for every pot, but I wasn't so sure.

Much to my chagrin, her hands were the size of catcher's mitts.

As the exam came to a close, the doctor called the receptionist into the exam room. I figured this signaled the end of the exam. *I'm safe*, I thought. When the pretty, young receptionist came in and closed the door, the doctor instructed me to drop my pants, put my elbows on the table, and relax. I knew what was going to happen next: it's prostate time, and of course, all the orifices in my body instantly constricted. Relaxing was not an option.

Eyeing the receptionist, I asked if an audience was truly necessary. The doctor said, "It's for my own protection, to ensure that you don't do anything inappropriate during the exam."

She should be so lucky.

"Seriously, Doc, this is embarrassing. I promise I will behave."

She replied, "Relax, Mr. Lentz. I have done this thousands of times. You have nothing to be embarrassed about, and my receptionist is a professional."

Yeah, a professional receptionist, I thought. I was not interested in her becoming a professional witness to me being violated.

And then the doctor's statement hit me, and I experienced a moment of empathy. She had done thousands of prostate exams. It couldn't be fun for her. I have soft skin, and while I have never waxed, I don't think it's a nightmare down there. She must hate the collection of hairy, pimply, smelly male butts she is forced to probe.

Finding my courage, I said, "Don't skimp on the Vaseline, doc. I've got a good PPO plan, and they'll definitely cover it."

My performance during the procedure resembled the elegant dance of a prima ballerina. I started with a plié, my knees bent over my toes and my heels on the floor. Then, I transitioned into a perfect demi-pointe, where the ball of my foot supported the full weight of my body. All the while, I made noises like a dying swan.

Just as it felt like she was tickling my tonsils, the pressure of her hand permitted a pocket of foul air to escape. The indifferent look on the pretty, young receptionist's face quickly faded. I definitely had something to be embarrassed about.

Mercifully, the doctor finished her exam. Unable to make eye contact with the pretty, young receptionist, I tried to preserve what was left of my dignity as I wiped away the excess gel. I thought, *Okay, Herm, you survived. Nothing could be more embarrassing than that, but it's over. That's the absolute worst that could happen.*

It was then that I heard the doctor say, "According to your chart, it's been over five years since your last procedure. I am writing you a referral for a colonoscopy."

To Be or Not to Be

I fancy myself as a writer. Who else but a writer would interject writeresque expressions like, "I fancy myself"? In a quest to hone my craft, I chanced upon the following posting from The Writers School: "Online Publishing Workshop. Looking for more publishing options? Wondering where current readers are finding material? Join us for a discussion about the online venues that publish and pay for stories—nonfiction and fiction."

Was this the milieu that I had been searching for? I was looking for more publishing options! I often wondered where current readers are finding material! I would love to discuss the online venues that publish and pay for stories! Screw my monthly blog post, where I not-so-subtly beg people to share my stories. I wanted to be published and paid for my toils.

The night of the workshop couldn't come soon enough. I was ready to embrace fame and welcome fortune. As I walked into the room, the instructor greeted me, looked at her list, and said, "Oh, you must be Herman."

I was totally caught off guard. Because I have a few semi-minor issues with my first name, my first thought was, *Oh Lord! I just celebrated my sixty-fourth birthday less than a month ago. Has my name finally become age appropriate?* As a kid, I was on the endangered species list; I was one of the few remaining Hermans still living. To keep the name alive, I thought I should be put out to stud. Standing in that community room, ready for the workshop, I realized that I was no longer the young kid with the old name. I must have looked like I qualify for the gin rummy tournament at Del Boca Vista Phase 5. What does a Herman look like? I guess at this stage of my life, it looked like me.

As it turned out, the only reason she got my name right was because I was the only man in a class with thirteen women. I counted myself lucky that the instructor hadn't said, "Oh, you must be Mary."

The class started with a meet and greet. Each class member introduced themselves and told the group why they were there. I was the second to last to speak. I opened with, "I didn't realize I signed up for a Women's Studies course."

Silence permeated the room. There was not a chuckle, head nod, or smile. Nada, nil, nothing.

The instructor cleared her throat and asked, "So, why are you here, Herman?"

I responded, "I don't want to be recognized posthumously," which went over about as well as my women's studies line. *Tough crowd*, I thought. *How do I save myself? Should I say my name is really SheDa Mann, and that I'm in the final stages of transitioning?*

The workshop was scheduled for two hours. We spent the first hour discussing publishing options, and then the instructor opened the floor for questions. No one said anything.

Finally, Herman/SheDa Mann asked about grammar and punctuation. "Will publishers reject pieces for that?" I asked.

She said, "Yes and no," then turned to answer questions from the other students.

A few minutes later, she came back to me. I said, "I have been known to use foul language in my stories. Will publishers reject pieces over obscenity?"

Again, she responded, "Yes and no. It depends on the publication. What do you write?"

"Children's stories" failed to garner the response I was expecting. To save myself, I said, "I have a website where I post my holiday cards and letters, which I hope people find funny. I invite you all to check out my website. That's www.Igottabme.com." When I noticed no one was bothering to write it down, I repeated the web address and said, "There is no E after the B. It's the letter B, then me."

Not a single pen touched paper.

As the class drew to a close, the instructor asked if anyone had already been published.

A smile flashed across my face. I wanted to respond, "Does a letter to the *Penthouse Forum* count?" A young, devil-may-care Herman might have said that, but SheDa Mann, sans balls, sat mute.

When the seminar was over, I realized that I hadn't found more publishing options, I didn't know where current readers were finding material, and I probably wouldn't find any online venues that publish and pay for stories. But I did realize how much I love my blog. Who cares about fame and fortune anyway? I write for my dear friends who share this journey with me, and if any of them feel like sharing my stories with others, I am forever grateful. Thank you. Thank you all.

The End

Or so I thought.

Thalia likes to critique my stories, and she told me that I needed a "middle" to the story, that the reader would not feel any empathy toward me. Something was missing. I saw her point, and now offer a middle, even though it's at the end.

The Middle

I couldn't understand why my jokes weren't getting the credit they rightfully deserved. I was upset. In addition to describing myself as having a great head of hair and a rapier-like wit, I consider myself to be Loveable Lentz. The thought that my lovability was not being embraced was disturbing and perplexing.

As I heard what the others were writing about, it occurred to me that perhaps my content was not compelling enough. After all, being colorblind is not that debilitating a disease. Deciding to buy a ring on vacation is not a crossroads moment. A prostate exam is not really a case of being violated.

Then I had a realization: it came down to the fundamental difference between men and women. Men have one and women don't. It is what makes men, men. And I thank G-d I was born a man with one. In actuality, and not to brag, I have a really big one. As much as women might deny its existence, theories abound on how they suffer with envy because they don't have one. Even Freud himself postulated on the subject and wrote a book about it.

I am referring, of course, to a sarcastic sense of humor.

Disclaimer:

To my female readers,

Ladies, before you take umbrage, burn my likeness in effigy, verbally beat me online like a piñata, or, in the ultimate act of disdain, return my book, please note that I did not say that women don't have a sense of humor. You married men, with all of our pitfalls; you must have a sense of humor (and sense of irony) to deal with us.

Instead, I merely inferred that women do not have a "*sarcastic* sense of humor." Frankly, I am thankful for that fact, as I shudder to think what Thalia would say to me if she were sarcastic.

Disclaimer to the Disclaimer:

Guys,

The above disclaimer was included strictly to help me maintain a semblance of marital harmony. You know how they can be.

The Flu Shot

I know that the flu is an extremely contagious respiratory illness that affects the nose, throat, and lungs. I know that it can cause mild to severe illness and can lead to hospitalization and even death. I also know that it can be prevented. The CDC warns that the best way to avoid getting the flu is to receive the yearly flu vaccine.

I don't want to get the flu. Even more so, Thalia doesn't want me to get the flu. When I'm sick, I constantly ask her if I have a fever. My nightstand becomes cluttered with over-the-counter decongestants and antihistamines, sprays, and menthol rubs. I guzzle bottles of DayQuil and NyQuil, and then moan, "Why doesn't Vicks also make an AfternoonQuil?" Halls cough drop wrappers litter the floor. I slather my nose and upper lip with Vaseline after I have wiped them raw from blowing my nose. I don't want to be touched, but I demand constant attention. I want to be babied. I'm a mess. Thalia knew before we got married that she wasn't getting some big, strong, strapping man, and she was okay with that. But she had no idea that she would have to deal with a pathetic man-child every time I got the sniffles.

So why do I ignore the barrage of public service announcements and dire warnings that are continuously spewed on the evening news? Why do I refuse to get vaccinated?

Well, I used to do my part and get a flu shot every year. The company I worked for was in the health care industry and every fall before flu season, they would send a nurse to the executive office to inoculate the staff. During my first year with the company, a nurse walked into my office and informed me that she was there to administer my flu shot. The company was not usually known for its generosity, so I was surprised that they were actually offering a perk to the staff. I'd never had a flu shot before, but it seemed like the responsible thing to do, so I agreed.

The nurse shut the door and started preparing the syringe. I rolled up my sleeve, but she stopped me and said, "No, no, no, not in the arm. I'll need you to take your pants off, sir."

As I unzipped my pants, I smiled and said, "I thought you were here to give me a flu shot."

With an exasperated sigh, she explained that the gluteus muscle in the buttocks is preferred for flu shots.

"What does that mean? I don't think I have any muscles in my butt."

"It's a large, fleshy area that is easier to work with."

Deflated, I asked, "Are you saying that I have a big butt?"

She shook her head, clearly not amused by my antics. She patiently explained why the buttocks were a better injection site and seemed eager to get on to business.

I was embarrassed. *What a rookie mistake. Of course it's a butt shot; everyone knows that.* "Okay, that makes sense. Thank you."

"And by the way, you have a nice butt."

"Mm-hmm," was the best response I could come up with, being a happily married man. The rest of the visit went off without a hitch, I thanked her, and she left.

For the next eight years, it was the same nurse and the same process: we'd have some light banter, a little harmless flirtation when I asked if my butt was still nice, and then she'd give me the shot. Then, in the ninth year, a different nurse walked into my office. She told me that the other nurse left the company, and she would be administering my flu shot. It wasn't my first rodeo, so while she prepared the syringe, I prepared for the shot.

The silence of my office was broken by a loud scream when the nurse turned around and saw me leaning against my desk with my pants around my ankles. Startled, I screamed back. Was it a horror show back there? Did I require some manscaping? Or worse, did I have an anal fissure or an abscess that was about to blow?

"What the hell are you doing?" she yelled. "Pull up your pants at once!"

"What's the problem? I'm ready for my flu shot."

She hurried to pack up her bag, and as she was rushing out the door, she said, "Flu shots are given in the arm."

Panicking, I said, "No, you're wrong! Everyone knows that a flu shot should go into the glutton area, you know, the large, fatty part of your ass!"

Later that day, human resources interrogated me about my deviant behavior. I was indignant at being unjustly accused, arguing that we had followed the same procedure every year. I said, "Go ask any of the other men in the executive office. They'll all corroborate my story."

The next day, I was summoned to a mandatory meeting in the conference room with all the other male executives. Scanning the room, I noticed the comb-overs, bad hair pieces, and glistening, bald domes. It looked like the other executives were there to pose for the "before" shot for the next commercial for Hair Club for Men.

In that moment, I realized that I had been a boy toy for all those years. With my great head of hair and nice butt, I was the exception; everyone else got their shot in the arm.

The nurse registered a formal complaint, and HR put an incident report in my employee file. To prevent a potential lawsuit, the entire company was required to attend two days of sexual harassment training. I heard that the course was very informative, but I didn't participate. I was home with the flu.

The Interview

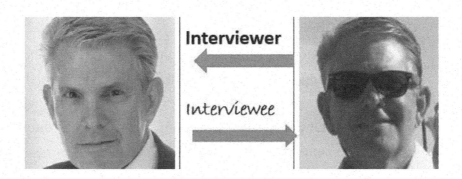

Interviewer

Interviewee

Thank you for coming in today. I hear you have a big announcement to make. Let me just quickly check my notes. You're sixty-six years old, you have been married for forty-one years, you have two married sons, five grandchildren, and you are here today to announce that you are coming out.

Turn over your index card, you idiot. I am here to announce that I am coming out with my first book.

Oh, sorry. I think the other story would be a lot more interesting.

Why did I agree to do this?

Okay, let's start again. You have what you think is a really big announcement: you are coming out with your first book. According to you, this is what the world has been waiting for. Not a cure for cancer or an end to war and hunger, which would be really big announcements to me. But I guess to you, your book is just as important. So, Herman, tell me about your momentous book.

Please don't call me Herman.

That's your name, isn't it? Who do you think you are? Prince? Should I refer to you as the author formerly known as Herman?

You know very well that I have issues with my first name.

With everything you have accomplished in your life, you still have issues with your name. Don't you think that might be a more interesting topic for us to discuss than your book?

No, I don't. How do you like *your* name?

Touché. Okay, the name is taboo. Let's try this again. You're coming out with a book, truly fascinating. Is this your first book? Oh, sorry, you already said that. Why publish a book now?

I don't want to be recognized posthumously.

Look at you, Mr. Writer, "posthumously." Really leaning heavily on the thesaurus function in Microsoft Word, aren't you? Or perhaps I should say that you have a predilection for laboriously exploiting the phrasebook application in Microsoft's word processing program.

Oy.

I see in my notes that you started your writing career with a website called Holidayrapping. Is it okay to call the website by its name, or are you going to get pissy about that also?

Holidayrapping was the title of my 1994 holiday card. Jimmy and Jonathon were dressed as rappers, wearing XXXL white sweatshirts, bling, pants halfway down their tuchuses, standing in a Run-DMC-like pose in front of a wall of wrapping paper. It was a really fun picture.

Yes, I wanted to talk about your holiday cards. They aren't the typical cards that everyone sends out. Tell me about them.

When my kids were babies, I wanted to send out holiday cards but wasn't a fan of the whole corporate, Hallmark concept. There's a lack of originality and they are designed for the unwashed masses. I wanted something different. In the beginning, my cards were harmless, cute pictures of the kids, coupled with a bad pun. It was only in later years that I started taking more risks.

Where do you get your ideas?

Michelangelo was quoted as saying that when he looked at a piece of marble, the marble would talk to him and tell him what was inside of it. All he did was free what was waiting to get out. I look at a picture and . . .

Wait a second. First of all, that is not a quote. It's an interesting anecdote, but it's not a quote. More disturbingly, are you really comparing yourself to Michelangelo Buonarroti, painter of the Sistine Chapel fresco, sculptor of the David and the Pietà? I suspect you have more in common with Miguel Angelo Lopez, my gardener.

How creative a gardener is Miguel?

He comes once a week and mows, trims the hedges, and pulls weeds. He's good but he is a gardener for G-ds sake. That's not the point. Okay, let's try again, where do you get your ideas from?

Honestly, my ideas come from . . .

Well, I would prefer that you don't lie. So yes, *honestly* tell me, where do you get your ideas?

It's just an expression.

I'll ask again and tell me honestly: where do you get your ideas?

Life gives me ideas. There are ideas all around us, waiting to be discovered. Or as Michelangelo the sculptor was fond of saying, "waiting to get out." Just the other day, I read the subject line of an email and thought it would make a great theme for a card. I didn't have a picture in mind yet, but I knew I had a theme. I worked on it for a few days and came up with a picture for the card.

It sounds like a lot of work. Why do you do it?

To tell the truth, oh sorry, let me start that again. I like to imagine that when you open your mailbox in December and see the envelope with my return address on it, you get the same rush, the same feeling of exhilaration that Charlie felt when he spied the Golden Ticket in the Wonka Bar. I'm referring to Gene Wilder's classic Wonka, not the Johnny Depp knockoff.

I prefer the Depp version.

Well, as the saying goes, different strokes for different folks.

(*singing*) **And so on and so on . . .**

Nope, not going there.

Come on, join me! (*singing*) **Scooby-dooby-dooby.**

You don't really think that I am going to sing, do you? I have a nasal New York accent; at best, I sound like a young Bob Dylan.

(*singing*) **Scooby-dooby-dooby.**

My apologies to Sly and the rest of the Family Stone. (*singing*) Ooh, sha sha. I am everyday people.

Thank you. Anyway, which is your favorite card?

That's a great question. Each year, while I am working on a new card, I love it the most. It's my favorite. Do you love one child more than another? I love them all.

So you're not going to answer the question?

I thought I just did.

Let me ask it another way: are there any cards that stand out from the rest?

Well, there are two cards that I think were truly inspired. One year, I dressed our Yorkie in a Santa Claus outfit and took a picture of him humping a teddy bear. The caption read, "You Better Watch Out, Santa Claus is Coming."

You sent doggy porn as a holiday card?

Yep. Thalia was horrified. I was actually forced to include two disclaimers with the card. The first disclaimer was that Thalia had no part in the creation of the card. To appease Peta, the second stated that no animals were harmed during the taking of the picture.

I can understand Thalia wanting to distance herself from the card, but were you really worried about PETA, the People for the Ethical Treatment of Animals, coming after you?

Oh, I was referring to Thalia's Uncle Peta in Greece. He just loves his cute little Yorkies.

I'm afraid to ask, but what was your other so-called inspired card?

I photoshopped the hats and curly sideburns that Hasidic Jewish men wear onto our Yorkie and our black lab and put them in front of a menorah. The line read, "Oy to the World."

I suspect that just about every Orthodox and Hasidic Jew might find that a tad offensive. What about cards that didn't work or were not as inspired? Care to discuss those?

Not really. Even Spielberg and Coppola had flops; it's just part of the process.

Unbelievable! Now you're comparing yourself to Spielberg and Coppola, or are you going to be glib and say Irv Spielberg, the orthodontist, and Tony Coppola, the butcher? Come on, there had to be some you're not proud of.

Okay, to be fair, there were two that were probably inspired by Miguel Angelo. Early on, I wanted to stop sending out cards, so I sent out a picture of three extremely heavy women belly dancing. The picture was taken from behind, and the caption was, "My Last Card, No Ifs, Ands, or . . ."

Wow, that's pretty bad. And the other one?

I'd prefer not to say.

I insist. But first, let me move my trash can closer, in case I get sick to my stomach.

I photoshopped the heads of my two Yorkies onto the bodies of Santa and Tevye from *Fiddler on the Roof*. They were arguing on a chimney: Santa said "Chimney," and Tevye said, "Roof! Roof!" And to this day, the tag line still haunts me: "Happy Holidays from Oy and Goy!"

What the fuck were you thinking?

I know. I know.

Okay, I think we've wasted enough time talking about your cards, so let's move on. You closed down the Holidayrapping site and started a new one in September of 2018 called I Gotta B Me. Tell me how you came up with the name.

This website was designed to house my collection of short stories. I know that not everyone will agree with or enjoy my stories, and that's okay. I'm making my own statement, and I feel that (*singing*) whether I'm right or whether I'm wrong, whether I find a place in this world or never belong . . .

(*singing*) **I gotta be free, I've gotta be free. Daring to try, to do it or die.**

(*singing*) I've gotta be me!

Now you're a vocalist. You should probably apologize to Sammy Davis Jr.'s estate while you're at it. Tell me about I Gotta B Me.

The site features my entire collection of holiday cards, and on the first day of every month, I post a new short story.

A new story every month? Wow, that's impressive. Kudos to you!

Thank you, that's very kind.

What are your stories about?

I write about things that have happened in my life, run-of-the-mill, ordinary stuff that we all go through, told from my personal perspective.

I have read some of your stories. You have quite a perspective. You have written about masturbation a number of times, bestiality, sunburned testicles, foreskin shots, drug use, prostate exams, midgets, gays, and lesbians. They aren't exactly the screen play for *It's A Wonderful Life*. Whose ordinary life are you writing about: Caligula or the Marquis de Sade? Your stories are not for everybody. Actually, they might not be for anybody.

Then I'll go it alone, that's how it must be.

I hope you realize that not everyone likes your stories.

I can't be right for somebody else if I'm not right for me.

Stop that, enough is enough with that fucking song. So, after three years, you decided to stop posting a new story every month. Why?

I had accomplished everything that I wanted with the website. In my journey as an artist, I wanted to take things to the next level.

Your journey as an *artist*?! Masturbation, bestiality, sunburned testicles, foreskin shots—that's quite a journey.

What else can I be but what I am?

Are you getting help professionally? And by professionally, I mean an editor. It goes without saying that you need help from a mental health professional.

Actually, I am working with an editor.

You're fucking kidding me. Really? A professional editor? Who is it? Xaviera Hollander, author of *The Happy Hooker*?

No, a legit editor. She has worked on manuscript evaluations, developmental editing, and copy editing for all genres.

Did you say "she?"

Yep.

You're working with a female editor and she hasn't taken out a restraining order?

Nope. Not yet, at least.

Unbelievable. And she condones your depravity?

I fear I might have broken her. After reading one of my stories, her feedback was that it needed more "dick jokes." Her words, not mine.

She actually told you to add more dick jokes?

Let's be honest, you can never have enough dick jokes. I did ask how many times she has asked for more dick jokes in all her years working with authors. I was her first.

And hopefully, for her career, her last.

Well, there is always my sequel.

You're going to offend a lot of people with your stories. You know that, don't you?

Regrets, I've had a few. But then again, too few to mention.

Oh no, you're not going to start with another song, are you?

(*singing*) But more, much more than this, I did it my way.

Please try to respond sans lyrics. Some people say that you push the boundaries of good taste way past the limits. How do you respond to that?

It's not my intention to insult anyone. I am trying to be creative and to bring a little joy to the world, all the boys and girls, joy to you and me.

So you're saying that you are misunderstood?

I think all geniuses and artists are misunderstood during their lifetime.

That's a bit pretentious, don't you think?

My point exactly. You misunderstood my response.

I give up. Let's just move on. You continually mention two things in your writing . . .

I know where you're going with this.

A great head of hair . . .

Yes, I am very vain about my hair. I realize I am blessed; I feel for the plight of the follicly challenged.

You do have a great head of hair.

Thank you, as do you.

You also reference your sense of humor quite often.

Actually, I refer to it as my rapier like wit.

Rapier-like, really? Based on this interview, you might want to unsheathe that sword of yours and sharpen it. It's been pretty dull so far.

Honestly, and I do mean honestly, I blame your questions and interview skills. I'm the creative one here. Who are you, my conscience?

You actually think you have a conscience? Let's look at the facts: You claim your sister is an only child, and you make a mockery of the fourth commandment to honor your mother and father. You're an observant Jew who married out of the faith, and you're essentially paying protection money to the Big Guy by joining a temple and paying exorbitant dues only to go twice a year on the high holidays. You have written numerous stories about members of Thalia's family that are password protected in your computer, and you've instructed your sons to hand them out at your funeral. Don't even get me started on what you've said about your coworkers over the years.

Please don't give away the premise of my sequel.

Oy. Do you like being married, employed, and having friends?

I do, but you have to admit that there are some really funny stories in there.

Seriously, Herman? You really think that you are *that* funny? That people want to hear these stories?

This interview is over. (*Herman angrily storms out.*)

Wait, don't leave. Come on! Herman, come back. I want to know more about your book, really I do. Hermie, HL, we can work it out. Life is very short and there's no time for fussing and fighting, my friend. H, Adolf, Mr. Symbol, come on, (*singing*) We got to live together, ooh sha sha!

Acknowledgements

To my wife, Thalia – my muse. The loving brunt of many of my stories, all written with love, affection, and wonderment at the incredible and multitalented person that you are. I can only make you laugh because you make me happy and secure enough to be funny.

To my sons – James (Jimmy) and Jon (athon) – I could not be prouder of both of you. With the exception of the stories you tell about what you did while you were growing up that your Mom and I didn't know about, I cherish each and every one of our conversations. And, truth be told, you two are the only ones who can bust my chops on a consistent basis and get away with it.

To my daughters-in-law – Jen, who only wishes I would tell more stories about James's various adventures, and Allison, who has tapped out on a few of my stories after only a couple of paragraphs. While you have to live with them, with great pride and slight apology, I accept full responsibility and credit for your husbands' senses of humor.

To my grandchildren – Leila, Maddie, Logan, Olivia, and Cameron – you each bring me such joy and "nachas." I hope when you're all older and read this book, you will have fond memories of your grandfather, who you lovingly called "Bucky."

To my editor – Katie Lowery. Katie challenged me, and all of my stories benefitted from her guidance, pushing, and prodding. Katie, an editor with over 20 years of experience in all genres, had to learn how to speak Long Island Jewish for this book. I was afraid that I had ruined her when she told me that I needed "more dick jokes" in one of my stories. This was the first time in her career as an editor that she given such advice to an author. And in the end, she was right, so I added more dick jokes.

To my dear friends – "The Bims," who I have known since 1976. As the newest member of the group, I am still reminded of my prospect status, and I understand that my probationary period is still not over. Even though you guys refused to call me David when I wanted to change my name, your friendship and camaraderie means more to me than any of you can imagine.

To my cousin – Lena Cutler, who proofread my stories and was a strong supporter of my writing from the beginning. Lena read my stories before I even showed them to Thalia and would tell me honestly if she thought I'd get in trouble with my wife for a particular tale.

To Dr. David Kreiss for his many moments of Zen. I would say he is my friend, but he has boundaries he must adhere to.

To my friend and part-time mentor – Mike Farragher, author of *This Is Your Brain on Shamrocks*. After taking my first writing class with him, Mike told me that my writing was at a "bronze medal" level and encouraged me to reach for the gold. His support and guidance are helping me get there.

To my graphic designer – Paul Prizer, who had the difficult job of trying to come up with a cover for this book. I told you we would eventually have an "ah-ha" moment!

To my wife – Thalia (again), I still can't thank her enough, or love her more.

To all the people who read my monthly blog and sent positive feedback, thank you.

Finally, I would like to acknowledge a few people from my past, who I will not mention by name based on the advice of counsel, but you all know who you are. While you might think you know my opinion of you, you are definitely wrong; I think a shitload less.